DAVID CASTRO

Deadly silence:
black deaths in custody

Institute of Race Relations
2-6 Leeke Street, London WC1X 9HS

Published by the Institute of Race Relations
2-6 Leeke Street, London WC1X 9HS
© Institute of Race Relations 1991
ISBN 0 85001 038 1

*We would like to thank Harrow Council for Racial Equality for its
financial support for this project and Inquest for its generosity with
information and advice.*

Cover design by Arefin & Arefin
Typeset by Spencers (TU), 1-5 Clerkenwell Road, London EC1
Printed by the Russell Press, Nottingham

Contents

Introduction

One death is a death too many.

Too many of us* have died without cause, since first we came to work for this country in the post-war years, in the custody of the police, the prison system and the special hospitals. Or if cause there be, common to all three, it is the racist bias that has been woven into, and become an inextricable part of, the culture and administration of these 'services'.

That is not to say that all wrong-doers, prisoners and psychiatric patients are not a citizenry apart, but that black wrong-doers, prisoners, psychiatric patients are, by virtue merely of their blackness, rendered an under-class of that already under-privileged citizenry. Black vagrants are even more readily than their white counterparts the sport and playthings of macho white policemen. Young blacks are frequently stopped and questioned on the basis of no more than a generalised suspicion that if they are black and young and on the streets they can be up to no good. And the way that blacks are subjected to violent arrest stems from another presumption: that blacks are violent and aggressive by nature and must, from the outset, be dealt with violently and aggressively. Violence is the only language they understand, and it is time they knew who was boss.

The contempt for blacks on the streets is carried into the contempt for blacks in their homes, for black family life. The black man's home is not his castle, even less the black woman's hers. There is nothing inviolable about the black family.

And prisons presume those presumptions: the statistics tell them that all blacks are potential criminals, the sentencing carries the conviction, it is no longer a matter of prejudice. The proof is in the numbers. The system is justified, it closes in on itself, it brooks no interference from outside – the indifference to black life becomes a fact of prison life. Suicide offers the only release.

If prisons are of their very nature closed-in systems, special hospitals are the demesne of the specialists – and to question their diagnosis of the 'mentally ill' is itself an act of madness. And yet, when it comes to young black men, the evidence is of a marked tendency towards diagnoses based on racial stereotypes rather than on individual case histories.

---

* By 'us', I mean black people generally. But black people who die in custody are predominantly Afro-Caribbean.

Racial diagnosis, it would appear, over-rides clinical diagnosis. Thus, young Afro-Caribbeans, who exhibit what is considered odd or anti-social behaviour, are commonly diagnosed as schizophrenic – schizophrenia being the disease that blacks are supposed to suffer from disproportionately, either because of some genetic reason or because West Indian family and/or child-rearing patterns create a cultural or ethnic deficit amongst black people as a whole. Little attempt is made to seek the cause of the 'patient's' behaviour in his (and invariably it's a he) particular history or the anomie visited on him by a racist society. Instead, the 'illness' which might well have been caused by the individual's inability to bear the brutal brunt of racism is further compounded by the racism implicit in the diagnosis and cure. And, so far from getting the care he needs, the patient is even further entered into a syndrome of un-caring from which his 'illness' first sought escape. The only escape now is the last. The cycle of discrimination, deprivation and death is complete.

But how do the police, the prisons and the special hospitals get away with it year after year? How does the bias against blacks work itself into the system? How does the culture of racism become policy?

To one extent or another, each of these services is unaccountable to the public in one way or another. And to the extent that they are unaccountable, inaccessible, specialised, to that extent is their power made more absolute. When such institutional power sediments into the hands of individual policemen, prison officers, hospital warders, the service becomes sclerosed against the public.

The structure of the services themselves further adds to that hardening. Ranked, like the army, in a strict hierarchy of command, they too tend to cultivate an ethos of phoney camaraderie by closing ranks when under attack. In the event, the chain of command becomes a chain of cover-up.

To the extent that the police are more immediately in the community, they are that much more vulnerable to public censure. But the lack of an independent complaints system has hindered a real and continuing openness to public scrutiny, never mind accountability, and led instead to the setting up of cosmetic race relations committees (to show 'liaison') and to public relations exercises (to forestall criticism). The public, however, and the black communities in particular, continue to break into this closed system with pickets and protests and people's inquiries.

Prisons and special hospitals, on the other hand, are a world apart, where the wardens are kings and the governor plays God over the lives of prisoners – moving them around as they please, deciding their present and future condition, withholding and affording medical treatment as suits their whim and driving them into insensibility through drugs rather than bringing them to their senses through therapy. Where the Board of Visitors is a sop to Cerberus and prisoners themselves may not bear witness to their condition lest their condition is made to worsen. Where none may enter except through the Home Office – and none may question except through the Home Office. Where, precisely because these are closed-in, unaccountable, hermetically sealed systems, racism goes unchallenged and fascism parades among the guards. Where black suicide is a cold statistic.

And the inquests afford no relief. The coroner is there to tell you the facts of death, not who was responsible for it or why. But even the facts are loaded against you. For the coroner's court is not an adversarial court where you have an equal chance to challenge the authorised version of the facts. Instead, it is the coroner who, aided by the police, is both judge and advocate, and controls the proceedings of his court. He alone has access to vital information stemming from an internal inquiry, but he is not obliged to divulge it. He alone decides which witnesses to call and in what order the evidence should be presented. He alone sums up and directs the jury, leads them – and tells them to choose from a restricted range of four verdicts, only one of which, 'unlawful killing', allows the relatives of the deceased a real chance to reopen the case with a view to prosecution and/or compensation. But such a direction to the jury is observed more in the breach.

Out of 75 cases of black deaths in custody recorded here, only one has resulted in a prosecution (of the police) and only in one has the family of the deceased received compensation.

The rest is silence. Black deaths do not have a good press, especially when they occur in the custody of our custodians. The media leads the public to believe that our guardians can do no wrong. Racism leads them to believe that blacks can do no right. The silence of the custodial system is compounded by the silences of racism.

We have chosen to break that silence.

A. Sivanandan

CHAPTER 1

Deaths and the police

Black people experience racism in the criminal justice system not just as a set of statistics or as generalised discrimination, but with a deep sense of fear at any point at which they, or members of their communities, come into contact with the custodians of the law. They know that at any stage – whether it is in their daily contact with the police on the streets, or during the course of police raids on their homes or communities, or at the time of arrest or being held in custody at police stations, or while being transported in police or prison vans, or in prison on remand or for sentence or awaiting deportation, or in hospital where they have been 'committed' under the law, or even while in the precincts of the courts of justice – the black person may be subjected to physical injury or neglect, leading in some cases to death.

And when such incidents occur – as they seem to do with increasing frequency – the black community's sense of fear and foreboding turns to outrage, not just at the unnecessary death of one of their brothers or sisters, mothers or fathers, sons or daughters, but also at the denial of information or explanation by those in authority at every level. Or, even worse, they are confronted with official disinformation, through which the death is explained away as 'accidental' or a 'misadventure' or even the fault of the victim, because of his or her behaviour, drunkenness, abuse of drugs, or mental or physical condition. The family and the community then face a long struggle – through the official channels of police complaints, inquests, inquiries and civil court actions, and the unofficial ones of protest and campaigning – to get those in authority to acknowledge their lack of care, their failure of custodianship.*

On patrol

As our evidence to the Royal Commission on Criminal Procedure and our further researches on policing have shown, black areas are overpoliced, black events are coercively policed, black people are associated with particular crimes and then subjected to particular policing tactics by special units.[1] Black individuals, particularly if they are young or vulnerable, are ready targets for a more generalised denial of rights and harassment.

---

* Inquest was set up precisely for this reason in 1981 following the deaths of Richard Campbell and Blair Peach.

David Oluwale[2]* knew this from the day he first landed in Britain in 1949 from the cargo ship *Temple Star*. On his arrival in Hull, he was immediately sent to prison for 28 days because he was a stowaway who couldn't pay his £50 passage from Nigeria.

His ambition, like so many of his fellow black migrants in the immediate post-war period, was to study in Britain, to become an engineer, but he was unable to secure a place in technical college and eventually took up employment as a foundry labourer. He is remembered by those who knew him in the early 1950s in Leeds as a 'popular young guy, sharp dresser, excellent dancer'.[3] But he and his contemporaries also found that Leeds was a very hostile place for blacks.

> We had three natural enemies: the Labour Exchange, the landlord and the police. A lot of us gave up – just bothered about clothes, dancing and girls. Not this David Oluwale, he was always trying. The police were the biggest problem, whatever we did, we couldn't avoid them. Sometimes they would stop us two or three times between the city centre and Chapeltown – especially late at night. If we argued, they would run us in for obstruction or something – anything. Then they would charge us with something bigger, either drugs or assault – and that would be that.[4]

It was following one such incident in 1953 that David Oluwale, by this time living with a white woman and their two children, was convicted, at the age of 22, of disorderly conduct, assaulting the police and damaging a police uniform, and sentenced to three months' imprisonment.

In fact, David Oluwale was not to be freed from 'custody' for eight years. At the end of his sentence, rather than being released, he was committed by the prison authorities to a mental hospital at High Royds, near Leeds. His eventual release in 1961 followed the Mental Health Act 1959, with its policy of removing from hospital those deemed not to be dangerous and capable of looking after themselves and placing them in 'community care' with their families or in hostels. But David Oluwale was considered 'unsuitable' for the local authority hostel designated under the 1959 Act and, now without family, was left to wander the streets and sleep rough, a life that brought him into frequent contact with the 'law'. Over the next few years, he was subjected to a series of arrests and jail sentences for various offences: six months for malicious wounding, 30 days for disorderly conduct, 14 days for being drunk and disorderly and, in 1965, another conviction for assaulting the police

---

* The individual cases described throughout this book have been included because, on the basis of the facts particular to each case, they seem to us to raise matters of concern in their own right. However, no specific case should be read, or is intended by us to be read, as illustrating or otherwise relating in any way to the general comments contained in any of the introductory sections.

following which he was again committed by the prison authorities to a mental hospital. Released on to the streets once more, he was repeatedly arrested and charged with such offences as 'wandering abroad' (under the Vagrancy Act 1824), disorderly conduct, and indecent exposure (for urinating in public), and received a further string of prison sentences ranging from 28 to 146 days.

David Oluwale was clearly a 'nuisance' to the authorities, as they passed him from the courts, to prison, sometimes hospital, and back on to the streets only to be arrested again and again. But he also became a target for a more vicious form of 'treatment' at the hands of two white Leeds policemen, Inspector Geoffrey Ellerker and Sergeant Mark Kitching, who let it be known at their local station that if Oluwale was sighted they were to be called out to deal with him. In August 1968, the two officers were seen beating Oluwale up in the doorway of the Bridal Shop where he had been found sleeping, and, when he tried to escape, he was tackled, bundled into a passing police patrol car, driven to a village seven miles outside the city and abandoned. Later the same month officers again drove Oluwale out of town to Middleton Wood and left him there, 'down in the jungle where he belonged'.[5] On other occasions, Ellerker and Kitching were seen beating Oluwale after kicking him to the ground and hitting him around the head and shoulders, and Kitching was also witnessed urinating over him while he was lying on the ground in a shop doorway.[6] Then, on 4 September 1968, the same officers arrested Oluwale and, while transporting him in a van to Millgarth police station, assaulted him with a torch and kicked him in the body and testicles. He was charged with assaulting the police and disorderly conduct and sentenced to six months in prison. Released in January 1969, Oluwale was free for just three days before he was arrested and returned to prison on a charge of disorderly conduct, a pattern that was repeated consistently over the next few months.

David Oluwale was to have his final confrontation with the custodians of the law, Ellerker and Kitching, on 18 April 1969. Another police officer was later to testify that he saw them beat Oluwale in a shop doorway:

> I heard blows being struck. I saw Oluwale run out of the doorway covering his head with his arms. I saw Kitching and Ellerker come out. They were smiling. They seemed quite contented with themselves.[7]

Two civilian witnesses later saw two police officers chasing Oluwale along the banks of the River Aire. That night, Oluwale's body was dragged from the same river, and an inquest a month later ended with the simple verdict that he had been 'found drowned'.

It was only after Ellerker was convicted of another offence that his and Kitching's campaign of harassment against Oluwale came to light and they were tried in 1971 for his manslaughter, and for assault and perjury for making a false notebook entry following one of their attacks on him. At their trial, prosecuting counsel said of their treatment of Oluwale in the months preceding his death that they 'hounded him, harassed him, assaulted him, teased him cruelly, and made a torment of his life'.[8] But the judge took a different view in his summing up, portraying Oluwale as a 'menace to society, a nuisance to the police, a frightening apparition to come across at night' and commending the police to the jury for doing their best 'to enable people like you and me to sleep in our beds in safety'.[9] Ellerker and Kitching were acquitted on the charges of manslaughter and perjury but convicted of various assaults on Oluwale and sentenced to two and three years in prison.

Nearly two decades after Oluwale's death in Leeds, a young black man, **Derek Buchanan**,[10] was found drowned in 1988 in the River Colne in the neighbouring Yorkshire town of Huddersfield. This followed an incident in which Buchanan ran away from two police officers after they had attempted to question him. The two officers gave chase, and it was initially reported that they had seen him 'jump' into a 'deep and fast-flowing' section of the river. Later, at an inquest, the officers testified that Buchanan had fallen over a weir into the river and instantly found himself in trouble, despite his being a strong swimmer.

And, in October 1987, another young black man, **Mark Ventour**,[11] was found dead in the River Nene in Northampton, two weeks after being reported missing. The original autopsy carried out by a Home Office pathologist found that Ventour had died from asphyxia caused by chewing gum lodged in his throat, although no explanation was given as to how his body ended up in the river. Ventour's mother claims that on the night after he first disappeared, a man called at her home to say Mark had been taken into police custody, but Northamptonshire police had no record of this. Later, an independent autopsy concluded that Ventour had in fact died after a violent struggle, in which he had been beaten about the head and shoulders and suffered extensive bruising to his face and back of his head. There was also evidence that an attempt had been made to resuscitate him before his body was thrown, with ankles bound, into the river. But no one knows to this day who, if anyone, was responsible for his death.

Raiding the home

*The callousness with which the police treat black people on the street is also carried into their homes. There appears to be a presumption that black families do not have the same rights as white families to privacy and dignity.**

---

* For raids on homes which did not involve deaths (including the maiming of Cherry Groce) see *Policing Against Black People*.[12]

Cynthia Jarrett[13] was born in 1937 in Jamaica and came to Britain in 1958 to join her husband. She had lived in Tottenham in north London for 25 years, during 11 of which she worked for National Plastics in Walthamstow. She was made redundant in 1983. She had raised a family of five children and, at the time of her death, had 10 grandchildren. She often looked after the children of friends and neighbours in Tottenham as well, and was an active member of the local Catholic church.

Mrs Jarrett's death came at the end of a chain of events which began when police decided to stop her son, Floyd, as he was driving his BMW car in Tottenham at midday on a Saturday. Floyd Jarrett was also well-known in the local community, having been a founder member of the Broadwater Farm Youth Association. The police say they stopped his car when it was noticed that the tax disc was five weeks out-of-date. But, as is commonplace when the police stop young black men in cars, they also ran a check against Jarrett and his vehicle through the Police National Computer. There was a slight discrepancy between the registration number on the tax disc and that shown on the car plates, for which Jarrett had an explanation; otherwise, the car checked out on the computer as not having been reported stolen, or been involved in any crime. Despite this, the police decided to arrest Jarrett on suspicion of having stolen the car and, when he ran away, they chased after him, tackled him to the ground and later charged him with assault on the police. He was subsequently acquitted for this offence (no charge was ever made against him in connection with the car) and awarded £350 costs against the police by local magistrates, indicating that the case against him should never have been brought. At his trial, the police testified that the engine number inside Jarrett's car had been filed down in a suspicious manner and that the chassis plate looked curved, both of which allegations proved, on inspection of the car, to be untrue.

Floyd Jarrett was held at Tottenham police station throughout the afternoon of 5 October, during which Detective Constable Michael Randall, who was off-duty at the time, heard about his arrest and took it upon himself to question Jarrett in his cell and subsequently decided to search his mother's home. His alleged justification for this action was that, from his dealings with many youths in the area, he knew that Floyd Jarrett 'was heavily involved in handling stolen goods' and that he had heard from 'reliable sources' that Jarrett was 'a major handler'. But there is a good deal of evidence to indicate that the search was nothing more than a 'fishing expedition': the warrant that was eventually produced stated only that the police were looking for 'diverse goods' and the search itself was carried out in a cursory fashion with one room that was locked at the time being left undisturbed while others, including Mrs Jarrett's bedroom, were searched. In fact, Floyd Jarrett no longer lived in his mother's house, having moved out six months earlier.

The search of Mrs Jarrett's home was carried out by four officers, comprising DC Randall and the three officers involved in the original arrest of Floyd Jarrett, with a district support unit and an area patrol car on standby in case of trouble. There is some dispute about whether the search warrant was obtained in advance of the search or issued afterwards. In any event, the officers entered the Jarrett home with a key taken, without authorisation, from Floyd Jarrett's possessions at Tottenham police station, although the police later claimed that they had found the front door of the house open. According to Mrs Jarrett's daughter, Patricia, during the course of the search covering various rooms in the house, DC Randall pushed past Mrs Jarrett and caused her to fall to the floor, breaking a small table in the process. The police officer did not assist her but carried on in the same room with his search, while Patricia went to the aid of her mother, helping her into a chair and telephoning for emergency help and an ambulance. A few minutes later, another of Mrs Jarrett's sons, Michael, came home and immediately questioned the police about the reasons for their search, informing them that Floyd no longer lived there. The police still continued with the search upstairs. At this point, Mrs Jarrett collapsed. Patricia and Michael insisted that the police leave the house and then tried to revive their mother, and subsequently DC Randall came back into the house and administered mouth-to-mouth resuscitation. An ambulance arrived and took Mrs Jarrett to hospital, where she was pronounced dead on arrival.

Medical evidence presented at the subsequent inquest indicated that Mrs Jarrett had been suffering from high blood pressure and severe heart disease, which could have triggered off death during any undue physical activity or emotional stress. But it was also said that, had the police simply searched one room and left the house, it was unlikely that this alone could have caused Mrs Jarrett to die. On the other hand, a push by a police officer followed by a fall, coming after the emotional stress of the search itself, would have been 'an important precipitating factor'. For their part, the police at the inquest denied that there had been any physical contact with Mrs Jarrett before her initial fall, suggesting instead that her upset had been caused by her daughter and son having been abusive, shouting and swearing obscenities at the police, throughout the time they were in the house. Counsel for the police even argued that Mrs Jarrett had suffered stress 'not by misbehaviour on the part of the police, but by the anti-police attitude of the children'.[14] These allegations against the Jarrett children were undermined, however, by the evidence of other police officers at the inquest, who had received radio confirmation during the raid that there had been 'no problems' and that the search itself 'was quiet', causing them to call off the back-up support of the DSU and patrol car. There was also the electronic timing records of Patricia Jarrett's phone calls for help, which showed that she was waiting on the telephone for two minutes, during which it was claimed she had been abusing the police in the house.

The coroner at the inquest gave guidance to the jury that it could only bring in a verdict of 'unlawful killing' if it was convinced that the police had intentionally or recklessly threatened or caused harm to Mrs Jarrett or deliberately put her at risk; if the jury was satisfied that Mrs Jarrett had been pushed but not deliberately, a verdict of 'accidental death' would be appropriate; but if the police evidence that no physical contact with Mrs Jarrett had taken place was accepted, the verdict should be death by 'natural causes'. If the jury was unsure of what had happened, an 'open verdict' should be recorded. In fact, the jury returned a verdict of 'accidental death', confirming its belief that a push by DC Randall had caused Mrs Jarrett's initial fall. But a later investigation by the Police Complaints Authority recommended that no action should be taken against any of the officers involved in the search of Mrs Jarrett's home or in the initial arrest of Floyd Jarrett, his extended detention, or in the decision to initiate the raid on his mother's house in the first place.

On arrest

One of the most dangerous points of contact between the police and black people comes during the course of arrests. As shown in the case of Floyd Jarrett, black people are frequently stopped and questioned on the basis of no more than a generalised suspicion, and when they protest about this or resist, the situation can quickly escalate into one of violent confrontation.

Clinton McCurbin[15] was a 24-year-old black man who had lived in Wolverhampton all of his life. An unemployed welder and member of the Church of God of Prophecy, he has been described as a 'loner by nature, not given over to violence and, being of slight build, did not represent a threat to anyone'.[16] On 27 February 1987, McCurbin went shopping in Wolverhampton's Mander Centre, a shopping precinct fitted out with a sophisticated surveillance system. McCurbin was in the Next shop when he came under suspicion of using a stolen credit card. The shop assistants, on instruction from the credit card company, deflected McCurbin's attention and called for the police.

Two police officers, PCs Michael Hobday and Neil Thomas, came into the shop and, when McCurbin resisted arrest, forced him to the ground and, with the help of a white customer in the shop, physically restrained him. PC Hobday, in particular, held McCurbin in an armlock around his neck for several minutes. PC Hobday was later to claim that his hold was on McCurbin's head and chin and not his neck, although he admitted 'in hindsight' that it may have caused McCurbin to lose consciousness and die. But a shop assistant told the inquest into McCurbin's death that the latter was having difficulty breathing when held by Hobday, and other witnesses said the police officer was 'practically strangling' McCurbin and failed to release him even after he had stopped struggling. Another worker in the shop confirmed that several black customers pleaded with the police to release their hold on McCurbin, and a third officer who arrived at the scene to handcuff McCurbin said that, although McCurbin's arm was totally limp at the the time, he thought 'he might have been faking it'.[17] In fact, McCurbin was probably dead by this time.

Immediately after his death, the police denied that McCurbin had ever been handcuffed and issued a statement that his death may have been caused by a heart attack induced by drug abuse. It was also falsely suggested that McCurbin had been a Rastafarian. In fact, separate post-mortems carried out by two pathologists confirmed that no evidence of a heart attack or traces of drugs were found in his body and that his death had been caused by asphyxiation due to the obstruction of his airway. A Police Complaints Authority investigation of McCurbin's death resulted in a decision that none of the police officers involved should be prosecuted or disciplined and, at the inquest, which was delayed for 20 months, the coroner was able to cite this fact in recommmending to the jury that 'it would be unsafe, wrong even, to find that the arresting officers misconducted themselves in difficult circumstances in whatever way'.[18] The inquest resulted in a verdict of death by 'misadventure'.

A similar verdict was eventually recorded in the case of **John Mikkelson**,[19] but only after legal action by the police caused an original inquest verdict of unlawful killing to be overturned. Mikkelson was even more of a loner than Clinton McCurbin. An orphan, he had been brought up and educated at Dr Barnardo's. He was later to make friends in the Windsor branch of the Hell's Angels and become the group's only known black member. On 15 July 1985, he was with other members of the group, first at their headquarters in Windsor and later at a pub in Feltham in Middlesex. On leaving the pub, the three men – Mikkelson, Alan Krafft and Martin Griffen – noted that they were being observed by police in a Rover and decided to drive to Krafft's parents' home nearby. They were followed by the police Rover into Bedfont Close where Krafft's parents lived, and, when their car stopped, the police Rover pulled up behind them. PCs George Renton and Richard Peacock challenged Krafft about his ownership of the car, while Griffen got out of the car and walked towards the Krafft house. Krafft claims he explained that the car was not his and invited the police to check out on their computer that it was not stolen. The police say he was evasive and that they decided to arrest him. Krafft resisted, and Mikkelson came out of the car to assist him. The police version is that Peacock drew his truncheon, struck a single blow to the heads of both Mikkelson and Krafft, and then put his truncheon away. Other witnesses, including Griffen, Krafft's father and a neighbour, say they saw Mikkelson and Krafft being hit continuously with truncheons by both police officers and also saw Mikkelson being held around his neck with a truncheon. Police reinforcements arrived in two panda cars, a van with dogs and a transit van containing a district support unit. A group of officers then surrounded Mikkelson and, according to the witnesses, continued the attack on him, some with truncheons, before he was dragged face downwards to the transit van and placed in it, in the words of Krafft's mother, 'like a lump of garbage'.

The police assert that Mikkelson's pulse was checked several times during the trip in the van to Feltham police station and that once at the station, he was placed in the proper recovery position. Krafft, Griffen and Krafft's father, all of whom were arrested and taken in separate vehicles to the police station, say that Mikkelson was dumped on the floor of the charge room and left unconscious for a period of at least 20 minutes without being allowed any assistance, and that it was only the intervention of a woman police sergeant that led to an ambulance being called over an hour after the first arrest. Mikkelson was pronounced officially dead at the hospital half-an-hour later. A pathologist, Iain West, found that Mikkelson had suffered brain damage due to a blow to the head and bruising to his body consistent with a struggle and having a heavy weight on his back, but that he had died from inhaling a small amount of vomit into his lungs. More significantly, West concluded that it was 'likely that Mikkelson was lying unconscious with vomit in his airway for a considerable period' and that his death may have been avoided had he received medical attention more promptly.[20]

Mikkelson's death touched off a chain of legal manoeuvring over the next two years, at the end of which the reasons for his death were still to remain unclear. An internal police enquiry was launched immediately, supervised by the Police Complaints Authority but under the supervision of a senior officer from the Metropolitan police, the same force as had been involved in the death. Alan Krafft was eventually acquitted by local magistrates on charges of assaulting and obstructing the police, and charges of obstruction against Krafft's father and Martin Griffen were dropped. At this stage, London Weekend Television decided to screen a documentary programme raising questions about the circumstances of Mikkelson's death, but it was prevented from doing so when the Police Federation, supported by the Director of Public Prosecutions, obtained an injunction on the grounds that the programme might prejudice the on-going internal police inquiry.

Seven police officers were eventually suspended from duty as a result of Mikkelson's death, but this was not until March 1986, after the initial inquest verdict that he had died from an unlawful killing due to neglect by the police. In November 1986, the Director of Public Prosecutions announced his decision that no criminal proceedings would be taken against any of the police involved and, a month later, following an application by the Metropolitan Police, the High Court quashed the initial inquest verdict on the grounds that the jury had not been properly directed by the coroner on the implications of a finding of unlawful killing. In his judgment, Lord Justice Watkins said he expressed 'no view on the strength of the evidence, except to say that another jury may not have found it compelling enough, especially if properly directed, to have found a verdict of unlawful killing'. But he went on: 'I am in no doubt that I would have directed the jury that it would have been unsafe to find that the arresting officers misconducted themselves in a difficult situation in any sense whatsoever.'[21]

It was in this context that a second inquest was held in February 1987. In contrast with the police, who were represented by a number of barristers, none of Mikkelson's companions on the night of his death could afford to take part in the reconvened inquest, which lasted over a period of eight days before an all-white jury. In fact, Alan Krafft was jailed for refusing to take part as a protest over the quashing of the original verdict of unlawful killing. At the end of the hearing, the coroner instructed the jury that there was no evidence that the arresting officers had used unreasonable force and, as a result, told it that it was his 'responsibility to take away from you the verdict of unlawfully killed by a positive act. I do not believe there is evidence for you to consider it at all.'[22] The jury duly returned a verdict of misadventure.

An earlier case in which a verdict of unlawful killing was reached was that of **Winston Rose**,[23] a 27-year-old former amateur boxer who died when being taken into custody by the police in Leyton, east London, in July 1981. Rose had previously spent a period in mental hospital suffering from schizophrenia, but had recovered. He had been made redundant in May 1981 and became depressed, imagining that his house was bugged and that people were pointing at him in the street. His wife, Thora, had arranged for doctors and social workers to visit him at home in order to persuade him to take medication and to be admitted voluntarily to Claybury mental hospital. When they visited, Rose started shouting at them – but there was no physical violence – and they later arranged by telephone for an order to be issued for his detention for 72 hours for observation and for the police to take him into custody. The police appear to have assumed that Rose might be violent, and 11 officers were deployed to pick him up, although no medical staff or social workers attended.

Initially, Rose locked himself in a neighbour's garden shed when he realised that the police had come to pick him up. The police surrounded the shed and called on Rose to come out, which he did, carrying a bible in his hand. He then tried to climb back over a fence into his own garden, when it is alleged that he kicked one of the police officers. At this point, another officer got hold of a dustbin lid and charged with it at Rose, who it is said grabbed the lid and hit the first officer over the head with it. The second officer then wrestled Rose to the ground and put a hold on him which caused intense pain to the bridge of his nose. The rest of the officers joined in to hold Rose down, and he was held in a headlock for several minutes until, in the words of one officer, his eyes were 'bulging' and he had been 'pacified'. He was then carried unconscious and with vomit on his mouth to a police van and driven away. Ten minutes later, when police realised that Rose had stopped breathing, they called for medical help. The ambulancemen who attended were at first prevented from giving him the correct form of resuscitation because he was handcuffed and the key had been lost.

After Rose's death, the Metropolitan police issued a statement describing him as a 'violent giant', weighing no less than 18 stones and being 6 foot and 6 inches tall. In fact, Rose was only 6 foot tall and weighed 12 stones. At the inquest in October 1981, the pathologist, Professor Keith Simpson, attributed the cause of Rose's death (like that of John Mikkelson four years later) to the inhalation of vomit. But he also told the inquest that the nose hold, headlock and pressure put on Rose's cheek during his scuffle with the police might have caused the lack of oxygen which led to his vomiting and death.

Despite the inquest verdict of unlawful killing, the Director of Public Prosecutions decided, in June 1982, that none of the police officers involved in Rose's detention would be prosecuted. Five weeks later, it emerged that the police had failed to inform Rose's wife and family of this decision, claiming that they had been told that no prosecutions would take place at the time of the inquest itself. Eventually, the Rose family took civil proceedings against the police and, in 1990, on the day that the case was due to be heard in the High Court, eight and half years after his death, they received a settlement of £130,000 from the Metropolitan Police. But no form of apology ever issued from the lips of the police.

Another black man exhibiting odd, rather than dangerous, behaviour met his death in a similar way. In 1983, **Nicholas Ofusu**[24] had apparently become very loud and threatened his teenage niece. She did not know that he was being treated at the time at the Maudsley Hospital for a psychiatric disorder and that, whilst normally gentle and lucid, he suffered occasional violent outbursts. Neighbours who heard an argument called the police. The police then gained entry to the flat by diving through a skylight and, according to witnesses, dragged Ofusu out via the lift, using considerable force. They did not call for medical help or attempt to take him to hospital. Instead, they handcuffed him and took him to Rotherhithe police station on the floor of a police van. There he choked on his own vomit and died.

At the station

A large number of black people who die in involvements with the police die at the police station. Here it is an indifference to the individual's health which can give cause for concern. Many of the black people who end up at the station (as with many whites) have not been arrested but found on the street, and taken to the station as a place of safety. But the place of safety proves unsafe when medical conditions are mis-diagnosed or ignored and when the intoxicated or drugged are neglected. Here, at the station, another presumption is often made of the 'suspect' black. Because 'drug-addict', 'drunk' and 'schizophrenic' are the labels police attach to black people, they can overlook quite serious and potentially fatal diseases such as pneumonia, hypothermia and sickle-cell anaemia.

Secondly, the labelling of a particular victim as drunk, or on drugs or suffering a mental disorder is often stressed in police statements to the press and public, prior to any post mortem or inquest. This, in turn, tends to deflect attention away from the behaviour of those who held the victim in custody and suggest that the victim was somehow to blame for his own death.

Tunay Hassan,[25] a 25-year-old Turkish Cypriot, was arrested along with his girlfriend, Seanna Walsh, in June 1987 during a burglary on a house in Hackney in London. Ms Walsh was later to claim that Hassan had suffered a beating from the police in the van taking him to Dalston police station: 'I said leave him, he can't talk English, you know. They handcuffed him and made him lie on the floor of the van and was lifting his head and smashing it down and putting their feet on him.'[26] It was later ascertained that Hassan had suffered bruises to his eye, nose and mouth consistent with a blow, and also to his back and shoulders. The police claimed there had been a 'slight struggle' at the time of the arrest, and one pathologist later testified that Hassan had not been beaten. But the evidence of another pathologist was that Hassan suffered 'numerous bruises and other injuries . . . consistent with having occurred in the course of a struggle'.[27]

At Dalston police station, the duty officer noted that Hassan did not look well and suspected that he might be a drug user. But, after an examination by a police surgeon, he was declared 'fit for detention' and placed in a cell. Six hours later, he lost consciousness and was taken to a local hospital, but, after another three hours, he was released from there and taken back to the police station. A police sergeant told the subsequent inquest that, on Hassan's return to the station, the police surgeon remarked that he 'wouldn't be suprised if he snuffed it'.[28] In his cell, Hassan fell asleep and, four hours later, the custody officer discovered that he was not breathing. He was rushed back to hospital, where he was declared dead on arrival. Seanna Walsh, the only non-police witness to Hassan's arrest, was found dead two days later, having taken a drug overdose.

Again, as in the case of John Mikkelson, the senior officer appointed by the Police Complaints Authority to investigate Hassan's death was drawn from the same Metropolitan Police force. Moreover, it was reported that this officer was active throughout the inquest in assisting lawyers representing the police and that he claimed to one reporter that protests over Hassan's death were 'all political. First they were trying to show he died because he was beat up, now they're trying to say it was lack of care. The real enemy is heroin.'[29] But, during the inquest hearing, it emerged that two empty bottles, which had contained methadone and valium, were found at the scene of Hassan's arrest but that this was not mentioned to the doctors who examined him as he gradually slumped into unconsciousness in the police station cells. The inquest into Hassan's death concluded that he had, in fact, died from taking addictive drugs, leading to his inhaling vomit, but that his death was aggravated by a lack of care while in custody.

The police were also to blame the death of **Jamie Stewart**[30] in July 1989 on drug abuse, in this case a 'lethal dose' of cocaine apparently swallowed while he was held in custody at Holloway Road police station in London. Stewart had been stopped in the early hours of Sunday morning driving his BMW car with three passengers, including a 16-year-old youth and two younger children, aged 14 and 10. The police said that the car was being 'driven erratically' and that this had caused them to pull Stewart up and question him about his ownership of the car. Stewart was also subjected to a search on the spot which, according to witnesses, included being required to drop his trousers while standing in the street. Eventually, the police decided to arrest Stewart and his 16-year-old passenger, leaving the two younger children to make their own way home from the incident in the middle of the night.

According to the police, Stewart became violent at the station during a further search and had to be restrained by several officers. At the subsequent inquest, one of these officers was to claim that, during the course of the struggle, Stewart spat out a plastic packet with traces of cocaine. Stewart was then handcuffed and put in a cell, lying face downwards. Shortly afterwards, it was discovered that his pulse had stopped and he was rushed to hospital. At the hospital, the medical registrar claimed that she was told by the police that Stewart had a history of epilepsy, had banged his head and been placed in a cell, and that they had tried to resuscitate him.

The next day, the police took the exceptional step of arranging a meeting with selected community leaders, to whom they reported that a pathologist had discovered large amounts of cocaine in Jamie Stewart's body. The authorisation for holding this meeting and releasing this information had apparently been given both by the coroner and the Police Complaints Authority in a supposed attempt to stop 'the spread of rumours among the community'. This action contrasts sharply with police attempts in other cases, such as that of John Mikkelson, to block publicity for independent investigations of deaths in custody in advance of inquests. The police action was seen by many in the black community as a contemptible attempt at massaging public opinion and was condemned by Stewart's family as 'both offensive and provocative'. The inquest, held in February 1990, concluded that Stewart had died from 'misadventure' due to an overdose of cocaine, but failed to reach any conclusion as to how his possession of the drug had evaded the police's notice during two separate searches.

These last two cases both involved young black men, a particular target of police 'suspicions' in inner-city areas. But one of the earliest deaths in police custody to cause concern to the black community was that of **Aseta Simms**,[31] the mother of young children, who was found dead in Stoke Newington police station in May 1971. Even though Aseta Simms was well-respected in the local community and was not known to have any drinking problem, the police claimed that she had been found drunk in the street and been incapable of providing them with a name and address. They therefore took her to the police station and placed her in the cell where she subsequently died. Police doctors later confirmed that she had suffered swelling and bruising to her head and over her eye and also reported:

> It is arguable that some people might die with this level of alcohol in their blood stream; but we have people with much higher levels who are still alive today. The bruising was consistent with someone falling about or someone who had been beaten. There was very little evidence that she had inhaled vomit, but this was not the cause of her death. I cannot truly say what was the cause of her death.[32]

An inquest recorded a verdict of death by 'misadventure'.

James Ruddock[33] was also arrested for drunkenness in February 1983 and taken to Kensington police station. He was lightly dressed at the time, in trousers and a thin shirt. He was placed in a police cell overnight with three other prisoners, who were given two blankets between them. Although Ruddock had pulled his trousers half way down his legs and was therefore subject to exposure, it was 12 hours before he was seen by a doctor who then discovered that he was 'cold as marble'. Hypothermia had set in and Ruddock died later at St Stephens hospital. Doctors found that he had not in fact been drunk, but was a sick man suffering from diabetes and sickle cell anaemia. The coroner at his inquest wrote to the Police Commissioner suggesting that if any prisoner was not conscious and speaking properly four to six hours after arrest, he or she must be seen by a doctor.

James Hall,[34] who was found by police in a phone booth in Battersea in March 1985 and taken to Lavender Hill police station, was also left overnight in a police cell without medical attention. It was not until four hours after his initial arrest, when he was discovered to have collapsed in his cell, that a doctor was called. He had died of a drug overdose and a ruptured spleen and was found to have lost four pints of blood internally. It was said at the inquest that a person suffering such a loss of blood would have shown obvious signs of distress, but the police maintained that they had checked Hall's condition every half-hour during his period in custody.

The case of **Michael Ferreira**,[35] who died in December 1978, is even more disturbing, in that he went voluntarily to Stoke Newington police station with friends seeking medical help after being stabbed by a gang of white youths. As in the case of John Mikkelson, the police did not call an ambulance immediately and spent a considerable time questioning the black youths about the stabbing incident. Ferreira died in the ambulance on the way to hospital.

Aseta Simms was not the only black woman to die in unexplained circumstances while held in custody at a police station. **Nenneh Jalloh**,[36] a Sierra Leonian, was arrested in central London in April 1987 for shoplifting and taken to Marylebone police station. She later fell to her death from the fourth floor of the police station, where she was being held. Significantly, a subsequent inquest recorded a verdict of death by misadventure rather than suicide.

Mohammed Parkit,[37] a 54-year-old Bangladeshi, was arrested just a week after Nenneh Jalloh by police from the Immigration and Nationality Unit at a central London restaurant where he was working. He, too, was taken to Marylebone police station where he was questioned about alleged forged passports. Mr Parkit had lived with his wife and four children in Britain for 22 years, during which he had never been in trouble with the police. He was, nevertheless, held in custody and interrogated for nearly four hours before being released on bail from the police station. On his return home, he complained that he had fainted while at the police station, and shortly afterwards he suffered the first of several heart attacks. Within 24 hours of his arrest, having had no previous history of heart trouble, Mohammed Parkit was dead as a result of six or seven heart attacks. The doctor at the hospital where he died said that he must have suffered a great shock or distress to bring on his death so suddenly, and an inquest held in July 1987 returned an 'open verdict', which indicated that the jury had not been satisfied that his death was attributable entirely to natural causes.

Elsewhere in police custody

Lack of care by the police can extend beyond the point of arrest and the police station.

Stephen Bogle[38] died in August 1986, a week after his initial arrest, while being held in the custody of the police in cells at Thames

Magistrates' Court in London. Bogle, an unemployed shoe-maker aged 27, was a known sufferer of sickle cell anaemia, a disease which could cause him to seem lethargic and to act in a bizarre manner. On the morning of 5 August 1986, he was taken ill in a chip shop in Clarence Road, Hackney, and a friend called an ambulance for him. When the ambulance arrived, Bogle refused to get in, and the ambulance crew sent for the police, who were told that a 'tramp' was causing a disturbance. The police officer who attended, PC John Evans, said that when he arrived and saw Bogle sitting on the pavement, he thought that he might be an escapee from a mental hospital and decided to take him into custody. But PC Evans then decided to run a check against Bogle's name on the police computer and discovered that he was wanted on a warrant, having previously failed to appear in court for an alleged driving offence and for possession of cannabis. He was taken to Leman Street police station and then to Thames Magistrates' Court, from where he was remanded in custody to Brixton Prison. It appears that he was later seen by a police surgeon, who thought him to be suffering from dehydration and advised that he be given lots of hot drinks.

At Brixton Prison, Bogle was seen by the prison hospital doctor on 9 August and again on the 12th, the day he was due to appear again before Thames magistrates. The doctor declared him fit for his court appearance, despite the fact that he had to be carried in a wheel-chair to the police van taking him to court. One prison officer said that the view at the time was that Bogle 'was in a state of paranoia, refusing to co-operate, passive, a malingering drug addict, or awkward, or just awful'[39] (i.e. anything other than the obvious, that he was ill). One of the police officers in charge of the van, into whose care Bogle was placed, said that he was told simply that he was a malingerer. He was placed on the floor of the police van, and when he arrived at Thames Magistrates' Court had to be carried semi-consicous into the building, where he was put on the floor in a cell.

It was only some time later, at the insistence of a duty solicitor appointed by the court who saw Bogle sick in the cells, that a doctor was called. He, in turn, immediately summoned an ambulance. But it was too late – Stephen Bogle was found to be dead when the ambulance arrived. A subsequent autopsy found no evidence of drugs or alcohol being involved in his death, and there were considerable indications that he had, in fact, died of a sickle cell crisis, having lost 10 to 20 pounds in weight. The inquest reached a verdict that he had died from natural causes, aggravated by a lack of care during the period of over a week in which he was variously in the custody of the police, the courts and the prison authorities.

CHAPTER 2

Deaths in prison

One might imagine that, once a person had appeared in court, and been either remanded or convicted to prison or remand centre, there would be time to evaluate and to attend to individual needs – and thus prevent more unnecessary deaths. One might also imagine that, given a secure regimen and a controlled environment, there would be no need to resort to dangerous levels of violence against individual prisoners. One might also think that the court procedure, with its capacity to commission social and medical reports, might ensure that those with psychiatric problems would receive appropriate care and not be left to the risk of self-injury or brutal control.

But, in fact, our researches show that more unexplained or unnecessary deaths now take place in prison than in police custody. And suicides now account for a large proportion of black deaths in prison. Suicides in the prison population as a whole are on the rise, despite a drop in the prison numbers. Between 1987 and 1990, 179 people died by their own hand in prison custody. In 1990, 51 self-inflicted deaths were recorded and in the first quarter of 1991, 12 prisoners killed themselves. Because of the high suicide rate, Judge Tumim, HM Chief Inspector of Prisons, was asked to head an inquiry. Amongst other things, he found that few staff had read the circular instruction issued in 1989 on suicide prevention (based on the prison working party report), that medical officers were sometimes too cursory in initial interviews with prisoners, and that the whole institutional milieu had to be overhauled.[1]

Our researches underline many of his findings. In particular, the inordinate delays in making psychiatric assessments or providing psychiatric care or finding beds in hospitals, coupled with a lack of communication between the courts, medical staff and warders, mean that prisoners who are clear suicide risks can be left without the proper care and attention until it is too late.

The police and the prison system have both been criticised for being closed institutions, a law unto themselves, not open to impartial scrutiny or public accountability. In both cases, there is the tendency for officers to close ranks, to back one another up when something goes wrong. But the police station still is, in a sense that a prison is not, a part of the community. You usually know where someone has been taken, it is your local 'nick'. You can physically go there to make enquiries, you might get a lawyer, you might alert a local paper, you might organise a local protest or picket, should you suspect something to be wrong. There is some pressure, however slight or informal, that can be brought to bear.

But the prison takes the individual out of his community both physically and psychologically. He is moved away from his immediate locale where he, his family and his history are known, where enquiries about his welfare will be made. His new environs are not merely miles from home but are in the control of warders who are, by definition, in an antagonistic relationship to him. And the contact that the outside world has with the prisoner is via a massive bureaucratic machine, run by a faceless government department.

Because of the nature of the prison system and the fact that witnesses are likely to be reluctant to come forward, because they are fellow inmates who are also at risk in the prison system, it has been harder to glean all the information surrounding prison deaths. Nonetheless, it appears that black deaths in prison custody do follow a very similar pattern to those in police custody.

Misdiagnosis

There are very close parallels between the death of Stephen Bogle (see chapter 1) and that of **Anthony Mahony**,[2] who died almost exactly one year later in August 1987 in Brixton Prison. In both cases, black men who were patently unwell and in clear need of immediate medical attention at the time of their arrests were, instead, treated as petty criminals by the police and the courts and sent unnecessarily to prison. In prison, they were subjected to apparent misdiagnoses; the danger of their medical conditions was seriously underestimated, over a period of several days, until finally they died.

Anthony Mahony, an unemployed painter and decorator with an apparent history of mental illness, was 25 years old when he was arrested after being found wandering in the streets wearing just a tee-shirt and socks. He told the police that he was not well and asked to be taken to hospital. Instead, he was charged with indecent exposure, held overnight at Kennington police station in south London, and taken before Horseferry Road Magistrates' Court the next day. There, he again renewed his pleas for medical treatment, but was remanded in custody for seven days. Because of prison overcrowding, Mahony was held in police station cells for several days, during which time the police apparently considered him not to be ill but a danger to others. He was transferred to Brixton Prison on the evening of 17 August. He was finally seen by a prison doctor, who found him to be physically well but mentally disturbed and advised that he be placed under special observation. He was locked in a special 'strip cell' where, on 19 August, his body was discovered, approximately 12 hours after he had died.

Anthony Mahony had died from viral pneumonia which had been present in his body for several days – a fact that, according to the doctor who conducted the post-mortem, could have been detected by a proper medical examination at any time during the period that he was in the custody of the police and the prison authorities. The subsequent inquest concluded that, like Stephen Bogle, Mahony had died from natural causes aggravated by a lack of care.

Armando Belonia,[3] a 50-year-old Filipino man from south London serving a sentence in Wandsworth Prison for indecent assault, also died in March 1988 of viral pneumonia, following a misdiagnosis by the prison authorities. In his case, however, the drugs he was wrongly prescribed for back pain were a major contributory factor to his death. Belonia entered Wandsworth Prison in January 1988 and suffered persistent shoulder pain, but early in March his condition changed and he experienced generalised weakness, was unable to take exercise and at one point collapsed. Yet, according to evidence presented by other prisoners at his inquest, prison staff ignored his condition, thinking him to be malingering, and, despite his reporting sick on several occasions, there is no evidence that he was allowed to see a doctor until 14 March. On that day, he was seen by a visiting locum doctor, who listened to his complaints of back pain and prescribed a course of DF118 painkillers. The next day, Belonia was discovered in his cell collapsed across his bed and could not be roused. He was taken to the treatment room and immediately referred back to the prison hospital, where he was seen by the same doctor as on the previous day. It appears that the doctor did not examine him or make any diagnosis but simply ordered that an X-ray of his back be carried out the following day. The only entry on Belonia's nursing record for the day read simply: 'From main prison, diagnosis back pain, can certainly put on the agony since when he has proved to be quite mobile when he wants to.'[4]

Belonia was placed in a locked ward of the prison hospital, where he passed the night in pain. Fellow prisoners reported that they tried to get help for him during the night, but that prison staff on duty did not have a key to the ward, which could only be obtained from the main prison building in an 'emergency'. Nor was there any doctor on duty overnight. At 6.30 the following morning, a hospital officer came on duty and recorded from information given to him by other prisoners that Belonia had 'apparently' passed the night 'in severe pain'. Three hours later, a hospital officer tried to take Belonia's temperature, pulse and blood pressure but found him collapsed. Only at this stage was he sent as an emergency admission to St James' Hospital in Tooting, where he again collapsed and was put on a ventilator. He eventually died at 5.30 the same afternoon.

Following Belonia's death, there appears to have been no internal inquiry conducted by the prison authorities into the matter, and at the inquest, held in July 1988, the prison doctor gave evidence that he had prescribed a normal dose of painkillers and had not been aware that Belonia was suffering from pneumonia. But a pathologist testified that the DF118 painkillers would have been lethal to someone suffering with pneumonia. The inquest returned a verdict of death by natural causes aggravated by a lack of care, and the coroner said: 'We have a man who dies from pneumonia and an overdose of painkillers and all the time he has been treated for backache. We do not have a satisfactory explanation for that.'[5] Because of this, the coroner reported the matter to the Wandsworth Prison Board of Visitors for further investigation.

Yet, when in response to this referral from the coroner the Board of Visitors decided to conduct its own inquiry, it was told by the Home Office that no purpose 'would be served by the Board enquiring into . . . the details of Mr Belonia's case which were looked at comprehensively by the Coroner's Court.'[6] The Home Office refused to instruct prison staff to co-operate with the inquiry and failed to make Belonia's medical records available to it. (His out-patients card had been removed or lost at the time of the inquest.) Despite this official obstruction, the Board of Visitors concluded that the prison did not permit Belonia access to proper medical attention; that record-keeping, communication between medical staff, and clinical observation in Belonia's case were 'inadequate to the point of non-existence'; and that the 'belief that the deceased was malingering precluded objective, clinical observation and judgement'.[7] Yet, the only official action taken following Belonia's death was not by the Home Office or the prison authorities but by the General Medical Council, which eventually struck off the doctor in Belonia's case for failing to make a proper examination or to refer him for specialist treatment and for improperly altering medical records.

There are also indications of misdiagnosis, leading to inappropriate treatment, in the case of **Akhtar Moghul**,[8] a 47-year-old woman from Pakistan who died in January 1987 at Holloway Prison in north London while awaiting trial for allegedly smuggling heroin into Britain. Her case highlights the plight of many Third World women forced by poverty into becoming drug couriers who, when arrested, find themselves in a totally isolated situation in British prisons. Such cases are a major factor behind the disproportionate number of long-term black women prisoners.

Akhtar Moghul was arrested at Heathrow Airport in October 1986. Although she spoke no English, it was evident from medical records and medication that she was carrying at the time that she suffered from a serious heart condition. But this information was not passed on to the authorities at Holloway Prison until a month later. At Holloway, she complained on several occasions of chest pains which, despite her heart condition, were attributed to the stress of her forthcoming trial. Then, a week before her death, she was put into 'strips' – a cell cleared of all furniture that is used as punishment for violent prisoners – because of her alleged 'aggressive' behaviour. It was also revealed at the inquest into her death that, when she was discovered collapsed in her cell, it took five to seven minutes to open the door because, as she was not considered to be a dire emergency, it was necessary for normal procedures to be followed and for two prison officers to be present when entering the cell. The inquest jury returned a verdict of death by natural causes aggravated by lack of care.

Inadequate treatment

Femi Adelaja[9] also died of a heart attack in February 1988 while standing trial at the Old Bailey, having spent 10 months on remand in prison, during which time he was denied essential medication. Adelaja was a black activist from south London, the founder of the Croydon Black People's Action Committee and the man who co-ordinated the defence of 15 black youths charged over the killing of Terry May, a white youth stabbed in a pub in Thornton Heath in 1981. May's killing had led to a massive police investigation, during which over 300 people were arrested. The Croydon Black People's Action Committee was also one of the first local black groups to set up monitoring of police activities in its area, a model of community action that was later to spread throughout London and other cities.

In 1985, Adelaja and four others were arrested and charged with fraudulently obtaining property, credit facilities and social security benefits. The case was one of the first in Britain to be based on computerised evidence. In fact, the police investigation and subsequent trial cost over £4 million. As Adelaja's solicitor pointed out, 'The whole case got completely out of control. It cost millions to investigate the potential loss of only £200,000 – an allegation which in any event was completely denied. When you add to this the history between the defendants and the police as a result of their successful activities on behalf of the Croydon Black People's Action Committee, it is understandable that they believe the police motivation was vindictive.'[10]

The trial lasted seven months, at the end of which all the defendants were acquitted, but Femi Adelaja was not to live to see this. During the course of the trial, in February 1988, he died, aged 36, at the Old Bailey of a heart attack. It emerged at the subsequent inquest that he had suffered since 1981 from sarcoidosis of the heart, a severely debilitating condition requiring regular treatment with steroids. But prior to his trial, Adelaja had been held on remand in prison for 10 months, during which time he continually complained that he was being denied these drugs by the prison authorities. In July 1987, he petitioned the Home Office, pointing out that the disease caused him breathing difficulties, fainting spells, and pain to his eye, chest and inner ear and that denial of the steroids 'could lead to heart failure or a further spread of contamination to my right lung, the result of either being possibly fatal'.[11] Despite the intervention of his solicitor, the Home Office failed to respond to this plea for treatment, and a doctor who examined Adelaja after his release on bail wrote to the solicitor confirming that 'there was no doubt that his condition had deteriorated markedly while in prison'.[12]

Richard 'Cartoon' Campbell[13] died following a month in custody in March 1980, during which time prison authorities twice refused to allow him treatment in hospital. As described by everyone who knew him at the time, he was a tall, slim, cheerful 19-year-old British-born Jamaican, who had left school in Wandsworth three years earlier and held down a job through most of the following period of his life. He had only twice been in 'trouble with the law', having been convicted for possession of marijuana and for being carried in a stolen car, resulting in a fine and a period on probation. His probation officer found him to be a 'pleasant, happy-go-lucky boy . . . with nothing to suggest he had mental illness'.[14] Prior to his arrest on 1 March 1980, he had managed to save £100 from his work as a carpenter and was planning a trip to Jamaica to visit his grandmother for the first time. He had also recently converted to Rastafarianism.

On the morning of his arrest, Campbell was reportedly observed for a period of three-quarters of an hour attempting to break into a sports shop in Brixton, south London, in full sight of a queue of people waiting for a bus across the road. Eventually, three police cars arrived on the scene and arrested Campbell, who refused to give his name or have his fingerprints taken when he was placed in custody at Brixton police station. Such defiance and refusal to recognise those in authority as a matter of principle is commonplace among Rastafarians. He appeared at Camberwell Magistrates' Court on the following Monday morning, 3 March, this time giving a false name, from where he was remanded in custody for a week and sent to Lewes Remand Centre. There is no evidence that at Lewes he was found to be anything but a normal prisoner. Two of his fellow prisoners there said he was still happy and cheerful and 'making jokes' as usual – his nickname 'Cartoon' derived from this side of his character. During his week at Lewes, his fingerprints were taken and from this time his true identity and background were fully known to all the authorities.

On 10 March, he was returned to Camberwell Magistrates' Court, where he again gave a false name and claimed that he was being 'framed' by the police. Because of this and his use of Rastafarian language, the magistrates decided to remand him for a further period in custody and to order medical and psychiatric reports on him. Although his proper identity had been established, his probation officer had not been informed of his situation, nor was he represented by a solicitor in court.

Campbell was sent to Ashford Remand Centre in Middlesex, which was described by one MP who visited it at around that time as a 'gloomy and unhappy place' with a medical wing 'darker, more claustrophobic and more congested' even than the medical wings of other British prisons.[15] Certainly, being sent to Ashford appears to have had a dramatic effect on Richard Campbell's condition and character. On his arrival, he gave an address of his 'foster parents' – in fact, an uncle and aunt – as his next-of-kin, but signed a form that they should not be contacted or told that he was in custody. Soon afterwards, he began to refuse food and fluid, except for a few spoonfuls of tea each day. Sometime after this, he was placed on a course of two major tranquillisers commonly used in the treatment of schizophrenia, and on 14 March he was switched to a single cell for 'observation'. Five days later, he was visited, for the only time, by his probation officer, who found him in a trance-like state and undernourished, so that the probation officer scarcely recognised him. The probation officer did not inform Campbell's family of his whereabouts.

On 21 March, an independent psychiatrist was called in to confirm the internal diagnosis that Richard Campbell was suffering from schizophrenia. This he did, citing as evidence Campbell's 'socially inappropriate' behaviour in seemingly looking at the window when being spoken to, his continued insistence on wanting to help the starving people of Africa, and his many references to 'Jah', the Rastafarian name for God. The medical examination also showed him to be malnourished, dehydrated and suffering from cardiac irregularities.

Two days, later Richard Campbell was found collapsed in his cell, with no discernible pulse, and was taken by ambulance to Ashford General Hospital where, despite his weakened physical condition, it is alleged that he attacked hospital staff and a prison warder. As a result, he was taken, handcuffed and on a stretcher, to a local mental hospital, St Bernard's, where the duty registrar examined him and found that, despite severe dehydration, he was mentally normal, speaking rationally and making perfectly good sense. The doctor offered to keep Campbell on at St Bernard's for observations, but refused to allow prison officers to stay with him because of the risk of disturbing the other patients. The prison officer refused to allow this and returned with Richard Campbell to Ashford Remand Centre. Within two days, the Ashford authorities again attempted to get him admitted to hospital as a psychiatric patient, under section 73 of the Mental Health Act which allows for such admissions without the authorisation of a magistrate. But the doctor at St Mary's Hospital considered him to be too physically ill to be admitted as a psychiatric patient and proposed instead to place him in a medical ward until his condition improved. Once again, the Ashford officials refused to sanction this and returned Campbell to the remand centre, where it was decided to subject him to force-feeding.

The decision to force-feed was taken without any consultation with outside medical experts or notification to Richard Campbell's family. This was despite a prison rule which required such notification at any time when a prisoner 'becomes seriously ill, sustains any serious injury or is removed to hospital on account of mental disorder'.[16] The prison authorities were later to claim that their failure to contact Campbell's

family was due to the statement he signed on his original reception at
Ashford, although, in the words of a consultant physician who gave
evidence at a subsequent inquiry, 'they were prepared to force-feed
Richard and this was a far greater infringement of his civil rights than
simply contacting his parents against his wishes'.[17] This doctor was also
highly critical of the method and conditions of Richard Campbell's
force-feeding at Ashford – involving the insertion of a tube down his
nose while he was held down by bed clothes – which he described as 'a
nonsense, and a dangerous nonsense at that'.[18] On at least one occasion,
the force-feeding caused Campbell to vomit and to damage his gullet and
lungs.

The force-feeding of Richard Campbell began on 26 March. He was
seen by the governor of Ashford Remand Centre – for the first and only
time during his 20 days detention there – on 30 March, when,
significantly, he was persuaded to voluntarily take some orange juice
and biscuits. At 7.15 the next morning, on the day he was due to be
returned to court, Richard Campbell was found dead in his cell, having
choked during the night unnoticed by the officer on duty. Later that
morning, as she left for her work as a clerk at the Ministry of
Agriculture, Mrs Jean Campbell, having last seen her son a month
earlier – his normal, happy, healthy self – was informed by his probation
officer that Richard had died in such miserable conditions in a remand
centre where she had never been told he had been detained.

The inquest into Richard Campbell's death was held in July 1988 at
Chertsey Coroner's Court. The coroner refused to co-operate with
solicitors acting for Mrs Campbell or to allow them to call witnesses.
After hearing medical opinion, following an earlier autopsy, that
Campbell had died of dehydration due to schizophrenia, the coroner
instructed the jury that it must accept this as the cause of death and went
on to say that 'your verdict, if you think that appropriate, would be
self-neglect'.[19] One juror later asked if a verdict of death due to neglect
by the authorities was possible, but was told by the coroner that there
was 'no such verdict' and that the alternative of 'lack of care' would be
inappropriate because the Ashford staff had done all they could, having
been 'landed with a patient who was extremely difficult'. The jury duly
returned a verdict of 'self-neglect', but without linking it to schizophrenia and also adding a rider criticising the adequacy of medical treatment
available at the remand centre.

Subsequently, an independent inquiry was held, under the auspices
of the Battersea and Wandsworth Trades Council, into the circumstances of Richard Campbell's death. At this inquiry, medical
evidence was given casting doubts over the diagnosis of Campbell as
schizophrenic and indicating that, with proper medical attention (as had
twice been offered by outside hospitals), his death was avoidable. In
fact, the autopsy had shown that he had had a pint of urine still in his

bladder, indicating that his kidneys were still functioning, at the time of his death.

Aggravated suicides

In 1973, another black youth, **Horace Bailey**,[20] died from hanging in Ashford Remand Centre, having been detained there for three months awaiting trial on charges of trespassing and theft. Horace Bailey had left school in south London in 1968 and, failing to hold down a job and being thrown out of home by his mother, took up residence in a hostel in north Brixton. He spent one period in borstal on a charge of theft, and when he returned to Brixton, it was noted that he had undergone a change of behaviour, standing motionless in his overcoat for hours in the lobby of the hostel. He became a drifter and in July 1973, while staying at a friend's house, a fight broke out between the friend and another man and the police were called. Bailey was arrested for holding a door shut against the police while his friend escaped. He was later bailed, but failed to appear for his committal hearing and was subsequently arrested again when found squatting in an empty house. Charged additionally with trespass and theft, this time he was remanded in custody to Latchmere House, Kingston, an annexe of Ashford Remand Centre, where he was observed by visitors to be in a very depressed and alienated state. By mid-November, after nearly three months in custody, he began to hallucinate about having killed someone, and he was transferred to Ashford Remand Centre itself where the prison doctor, suspecting schizophrenia, administered a major tranquilliser. Eventually, on 23 November, he was taken to court for an appearance with another defendant accused of assault. Although Bailey had instructed a solicitor, he was not represented at court and bail was refused; the judge did, however, criticise the length of time he had spent in custody awaiting trial. Returned to Ashford, he had further hallucinations about having killed someone and, on November 26, the prison doctor decided to arrange for him to be committed to mental hospital. But this intervention came too late – that night, Horace Bailey was found dead, hanging from bedsheets in his cell.

On 20 December, a 35-minute inquest was held on Horace Bailey before the Surrey County Coroner, Lt Col George McEwan (who was also to preside at the inquest on Richard Campbell seven years later). At the inquest, Father Andrew Grant, who ran the hostel in Brixton where Horace Bailey had lived and who had maintained contact with him during his detention at Ashford, asked, 'Why was the probation officer not called? She had been asking for medical reports persistently over several months. She was disturbed at his psychiatric state and found it impossible to convince people he needed this kind of help.'[21] This prompted the coroner to recall the governor of Ashford Remand Centre, who told the jury that 29,500 young prisoners passed through the centre each year. The coroner then told the jury: 'You can see that it is extremely difficult for the authorities to collect information.'[22] The jury returned a verdict of suicide.

The inquest on **Paul Worrell**,[23] who died in Brixton Prison in January 1982, returned an open verdict, despite clear evidence that he had hanged himself, an indication of the jury's disquiet over the circumstances of his death. Paul Worrell was a 21-year old amateur boxing champion from Plumstead, south London, where he was arrested for the first time in September 1981 for allegedly assaulting two people at a local pub. He later appeared at Woolwich Magistrates' Court and was remanded to Brixton Prison. Subsequently, a consultant from Guy's Hospital diagnosed Worrell as schizophrenic and in need of medical attention, and a bed at the hospital was offered for him. But, as in the case of Richard Campbell, the prison authorities refused to sanction this, considering Worrell to be too violent to be in an open ward. Yet, the same authorities appear to have adjudged him fit to plead on the criminal charges against him.

Despite the requirement that he be observed every 15 minutes, Paul Worrell managed, on 12 January 1982, to hang himself, having been left alone in his cell with sheets, towel and an extra shirt with which to make a noose. His family were later refused both access to the cell to inspect it and legal aid in order to obtain independent medical evidence on his death. The Home Office also turned down a request for a public inquiry to be established following the inquest jury's open verdict. Instead, his family were forced to go to the High Court to seek a judicial review of his treatment while in Brixton Prison, based on independent medical evidence of 'gross deficiencies in the quality of psychiatric care and treatment available to inmates' there and the testimony of one prison medical officer that, because of inadequate record-keeping and staffing, 'some suicidal patients are not been properly watched'.[24] But Paul Worrell's family lost their case when the judge refused to rule that prisons could reasonably be expected to provide the same quality of care as hospitals. 'In my judgment,' intoned Mr Justice Pill, 'the law should not and does not expect the same standard' for those in custody of prisons.[25]

The case of **Sajjan Singh Atwal**,[26] who died in Winson Green Prison in Birmingham in September 1988, demonstrates again how inadequate record-keeping and communications among the authorities can lead to fatal consequences for black prisoners. Atwal had been serving a life sentence for murder at Sudbury Open Prison in Derbyshire when, in July 1988, he absconded and was later re-arrested. A fellow prisoner testified that Atwal had earlier tried to commit suicide, and when he was returned to Sudbury, the hospital authorities there certainly considered him to be a suicide risk. One prison hospital officer told the subsequent inquest that he considered that Atwal 'was emphatically thinking of suicide. He was very withdrawn, flat and emotionless.'[27] Immediately, steps were taken to transfer him to Winson Green Prison where he could supposedly receive better medical attention. At Winson Green, Atwal went on hunger strike – his cell-mate said that Atwal had 'thought all his chances were lost' because of his attempted escape. As a matter of routine, he was isolated in a cell on his own where his food and drink could be monitored. Twenty-four hours later, on 4 September, he was found hanged by bedsheets.

Prison officers at Winson Green denied any knowledge of Atwal being at risk of suicide, and the doctor there, who had examined him two days before his death, also said he was not aware of this fact, explaining that 'anybody who had tried to commit suicide would have been taken to hospital'.[28] The original inquest reached the conclusion that Atwal had died solely from a lack of care on the part of the prison authorities, but the Home Office felt compelled to challenge this verdict in the Divisional Court, arguing that the 'lack of care' verdict should not have been put to the jury on its own, without reference to the other circumstances of the death. As in the case of John Mikkelson, this verdict, openly critical of the authorities, was quashed by the Divisional Court, and a second inquest had to be convened, which altered the finding to one of 'suicide in circumstances brought about by lack of care'. After the second inquest, the solicitor for the Home Office declared: 'This verdict is pretty much what we expected. I imagine the Home Office will not be thinking of any further action.'[29]

Since then, up to January 1991 when our research ended, five more young black men have taken their own lives in prison custody. In January 1991, 29-year-old **Delroy McKnight**[30] broke a piece of glass from his cell window and, telling his cell-mate, 'I've had enough, Mick, I'm going', he systematically sawed through the main vein and artery in his neck until he bled to death. The cell-mate raised the alarm and pounded and kicked the cell door to attract the warders. But, he told the inquest at Westminster Coroner's Court, it took 15 minutes for help to come.

McKnight's fate was similar to that of Atwal and Worrell. He had been diagnosed as suffering from acute paranoid schizophrenia and it was noted that he had suicidal ideas. His psychiatric care consisted of daily doses of largactyl. He was moved from Highpoint Prison in December 1990 to Wandsworth. His family were not told of the move, nor was Wandsworth informed that the move was intended to give him access to proper psychiatric care. His suicide risk was ignored by the medical officer on admission. McKnight was not placed in a special cell, nor put on a special watch. When he failed to turn up for his daily medication, no one noticed; when he stopped eating or washing, no one noticed.

The jury returned a verdict that he killed himself while the balance of his mind was disturbed and that the cause of his death was contributed to by lack of care. The lack of care exhibited in this case moved the coroner (who had also officiated at the inquest of Armando Belonia) to make a number of recommendations about medical care at Wandsworth and suicide prevention procedures.

Another category of prisoner seriously at risk of suicide is that of asylum-seekers, who frequently face the threat of removal back into dangerous situations. **Ahmed Katangole**,[31] a 24-year-old Bagandan man active in the Federal Democratic Movement of Uganda (FDMU), arrived in Britain in September 1986 seeking political asylum. He feared being killed if he returned to Uganda because of his opposition to the central government in that country – this fate already having befallen one of the leaders of the FDMU. Katangole was detained at a holding centre at Gatwick Airport for about a week. He was then able to provide the immigration authorities with a permanent address where he could live while his application for asylum was being considered. He was released from custody, after which he complied fully with all the conditions imposed on him regarding keeping the Home Office informed of his whereabouts. His case was taken up by the Uganda Welfare Action Group (UWAG), which was assisting him in compiling evidence on the political situation in Uganda to support his claim for asylum.

On 3 March 1987, when Katangole reported for an appointment with the immigration authorities, he was immediately detained and taken to Gatwick Airport, from where he was told he would be deported the next day. At the airport, he managed to purchase a bottle of paracetamol tablets and swallowed 20 to 30 of them, as a result of which he was rushed to Crawley Hospital. He was seen by a doctor, who subsequently wrote to the authorities at Gatwick Airport confirming that Katangole believed he would be killed if returned to Uganda and that 'this man took a potentially lethal dose of paracetamol while under extreme stress, and should he find himself in a similar position he would have no hesitation in taking his own life, using whatever method was most easily available'.[32] Although the hospital recommended that he be released from custody because of his mental state and contacted the UWAG to assist him, the immigration authorities removed him from the hospital before its representative could arrive. Over the next eight days, it appears that Katangole was moved from one place of detention to another, with UWAG trying in vain to locate him, especially to inform him that an MP had intervened and was now compiling new evidence to submit to the Home Office in support of his application for asylum. On 12 March, Katangole was sent from Latchmere House (now an immigration detention centre), where there were inadequate medical facilities to look after him, to Pentonville Prison, where he was diagnosed by the prison psychiatrist as suffering from 'reactive depression' (i.e., his depression was an understandable response to real events). The psychiatrist recommended that the care he required was 'political rather than therapeutic'.[33]

Within just two days, however, Katangole was said by prison warders to have 'perked up' and he was moved from a cell where he was being constantly monitored to one where he would be observed only every 15 minutes. In the meantime, the MP who had intervened in Katangole's case had submitted the evidence to support his asylum application by the Home Office's deadline of 20 March. It is unclear whether Katangole was unaware of this or had been told that, the evidence having been considered, his application had been refused and that he would be removed as a result. Whatever the case, he was found hanged in his cell early in the morning of 22 March. An inquest jury was later to decide that his death had been caused by 'suicide due to official indifference and lack of care'.

At least two self-inflicted deaths have taken place since Katangole's death at Harmondsworth detention centre. In October 1989, **Siho Iyugiven**, a Kurdish refugee from Turkey denied asylum in Britain, set fire to his bedding in protest and died from subsequent burns. In June 1990, **Kimpua Nsimba**, a Zairean claiming asylum, was found hanged. It appears from the two inquests that the detention centre, which is run by a private security firm, does not have to abide by the same standards as a prison. For example, there were found to be few fire extinguishers and no sprinklers when Iyugiven set his cell alight. And it transpired after Nsimba's death that the security firm was given no training in suicide prevention.[34]

Following violent treatment

Another immigration prisoner to die, possibly as a result of his treatment in custody, was **Bahader Singh**,[35] who collapsed in India in 1989 on the very day he arrived there following his deportation from Britain. He had been held for the previous six months in Glasgow's Barlinnie jail. During this time he was said to have faced racist abuse and violence from other prisoners, including being beaten by iron bars, kicked and punched, and he had had to be put into solitary confinement for his own protection. His death helped to expose the racist treatment faced by immigration detainees and led to the case of another prisoner, Vijay Kumar, who had been held for 11 weeks in similar circumstances in Barlinnie jail, being taken up by a Scottish MP and going before the Court of Sessions. There the judge, Lord Weir, ordered his immediate release and described the system of locking someone up for months pending deportation as 'scandalous'.

Anachu Anozie Osita,[36] a 28-year-old Nigerian, was being held on remand pending his trial for fraud when, in May 1987, he was due to be transferred from Wormwood Scrubs to Brixton Prison for medical treatment. He allegedly became violent while being placed in the prison van and it was decided by officers to restrain him using a body belt, even though the necessary authority for this had not been obtained from the prison governor. Equally, no consultant psychiatrist was available at the weekend to authorise the use of sedation. As well as being put in the body belt, Osita was handcuffed on each side and a plastic strap was placed around his ankles – one prison officer later testified that, during the journey, he was making a gurgling sound 'like something was stuck in his throat'.[37] He died in the van. According to the pathologist who conducted the post mortem, his death was the result of a lung disease aggravated by a lack of oxygen due to the restraint placed on him by the body belt. At the end of the inquest, the coroner, Sir Montague Levine, criticised the prison staff involved and told the jury that to return a verdict of death by natural causes aggravated by lack of care would imply that, in its opinion, the body belt should never have been used on Osita. The jury did return this verdict.

Just over three years later, the same coroner presided at the inquest into the death of **Germain Alexander**[38] in Brixton Prison, an inquest that was to lead to his demanding an immediate inquiry into the way in which acute psychiatric emergencies are dealt with both in police stations and in prisons, especially at night. A carpenter by trade, Alexander had come to Britain from Dominica in 1955. In 1987, his son by his first marriage went missing for five days before being found hanged by his own shoelaces in an empty toilet at Euston fire station. In the same year, Germain Alexander was diagnosed as a manic depressive, and on four occasions he was remanded under the Mental Health Act into hospital for treatment, although he never served a prison sentence.

On 4 December, Alexander, now aged 58, was arrested in the early hours of the morning and charged with assaulting three police officers after they had been called to a 'disturbance' at a party near to his home in north London. But, at 4.00am, he was released from police custody on bail, only to be re-arrested less than two hours later and charged with assaulting another police officer. This second arrest resulted in a violent struggle, with Alexander being laid face down in a police van and physically restrained by four officers. At Edmonton Magistrates' Court later the same morning, he complained to the duty solicitor of police brutality, both during his arrest and while being held at the police station, and the duty solicitor observed that the police were very hostile towards Alexander, who they warned was a 'nutter'. It was subsequently confirmed from police records that Alexander had indeed suffered cuts and bruises *before* he arrived at the prison.

Despite his record showing clearly that he was mentally ill and had previously been in mental hospital, the magistrates decided to remand

Alexander to Brixton Prison. On his arrival there, he was seen by a prison doctor, who failed to note his bodily injuries but diagnosed him as suffering from a manic depressive syndrome. The doctor recommended that he be placed in a single cell in the hospital wing of the prison and removed to a strip cell should he become aggressive. Early in the morning of 6 December, prison officers claim that Alexander became manic and threatened his cell-mate, although this was denied by the prisoner concerned at the subsequent inquest. No doctor was on duty at night – the principal prison officer later testified that he had not known a doctor to be called out to the prison at night for 14 years – and the hospital officer had no medical qualifications, despite his being in charge of 231 prisoners, most with psychiatric illnesses. A decision was made to remove Alexander to a strip cell, located down a 42-step walkway, using 'control and restraint' procedures. These involved officers donning riot gear and shields and using ratchet handcuffs on the prisoner. The doctor who had authorised Alexander's removal to a strip cell over the telephone later testified that, in hindsight, had she known that force was to be used, she would have refused permission until she had arrived and been able to administer a sedative injection.

Fellow prisoners who appeared at the inquest told of a violent struggle between prison officers and Alexander. They claimed that a group of five or six officers in riot gear rushed to his cell, where they removed the door from its hinges, dragged him out and 'bounced' him down the stairs. Then, it was alleged, with Alexander laid face down on a landing floor and handcuffed to the rails, he was kicked and beaten in 'a bloody fury'. Prison officers at the inquest gave contradictory accounts, some claiming that Alexander had walked down the stairs and others that he was carried, one admitting that abusive language was directed at Alexander while five others denied this. The official record showed that only three prison officers removed Alexander from his cell, although one testified that four were involved, and the doctor in the case confirmed that when she later visited the prison, she found the door to Alexander's cell lying off its hinges.

Alexander was left locked in a strip cell and was later observed through the door to have stopped breathing. The hospital officer on duty did not know how to insert a plastic airway into his mouth, and Alexander was taken to King's College Hospital where he died. The post mortem confirmed that Alexander had not only suffered a heart attack during 'prolonged acts of violence', but also that he had sustained injuries consistent with 'a violent struggle when the individual is resisting attempts to restrain him'. These injuries included a fractured bone in his spine, probably the result of a 'blow to the small of the back or the application of pressure, such as from a knee'; damage to three ribs; and two teeth lodged in his throat and a third sheared off at gum level.[39] Alexander had no history of heart trouble and his body showed no evidence of heart disease. The inquest jury returned a unanimous verdict that Alexander had died from natural causes aggravated by lack of care, and the coroner declared that he 'viewed some aspects of this inquest with much disquiet and concern'.[40] Germain Alexander's daughter stated simply: 'My father should have been treated properly as a patient in a mental hospital. He should never have been in prison.'[41]

CHAPTER 3

Deaths in hospital custody

*As the cases of Paul Worrell and Germain Alexander reveal, the penal system cannot decide, or is indifferent to, the question whether black men considered to be violent and dangerous are bad (i.e., should be criminalised) or mad (i.e., should be hospitalised).¹ Whichever is the case, the results of leaving the mentally sick in a prison environment have been catastrophic. On the other hand, those black inmates of the prison system who are sane but display a resistance to what they perceive as racist procedures (e.g., in their refusal to recognise the courts or in their objection to having their locks cut) are at risk to medical diagnosis and forcible removal to a psychiatric special hospital.***

Young black men who have committed no crime at all can find themselves in high security mental hospitals where they have even fewer rights than prisoners. Young black men born in the Caribbean are 25 times more likely than young white men, and black men born here four times more likely than young whites, to be 'sectioned' under the Mental Health Act – i.e., forcibly removed to psychiatric hospital.³ It is notoriously difficult to find a way out of special hospitals because it often depends upon the subjective clinical judgment of doctors, rather than any statutory yardstick or fixed penalty.

The most common diagnosis made of Afro-Caribbean men who exhibit what is considered odd or anti-social behaviour is that of schizophrenia. The cause of the behaviour is not sought in the particular history of an individual or the dislocation visited on the individual by a racist society. Rather, schizophrenia is considered to be a black disease – a disease that blacks suffer from disproportionately either because of some genetic reason or because family or child-rearing patterns have created a cultural or ethnic deficit amongst black people as a whole.

And the treatment is generally chemical rather than therapeutic. Psycho-analysis or group therapy is rarely on offer. Instead, drugs to sedate or alter behaviour are used as a form of control of black patients. Black community groups have advanced the argument that the black patient's perceived problem might actually be an altered mental state induced by hospital drugs (and especially combinations of drugs). But special hospitals like Broadmoor, Rampton or Ashworth, which are used for the 'criminally insane', those

---

* In 1979, just weeks before his release, black prisoner Steve Thompson, who refused to have his locks shorn at Gartree prison, was sent to Rampton Special Hospital where he was diagnosed as schizophrenic. Four months later, after legal action, he was given an absolute discharge.²

deemed dangerous to themselves or the public as well as the mentally retarded,
are apparently impervious to such arguments. Their regimens are, according to
former patients, more akin to prisons than to hospitals; control rather than cure
is their stock in trade.

Michael Martin,[6] who had no criminal record and had never been in trouble with the police, died in Broadmoor Special Hospital in 1984, following his forced removal down a flight of stairs by a group of officers using 'control and restraint' procedures and his being placed under heavy sedation. He had been born in Lewisham, south London, in 1961, one of five children brought up by his mother, a nursing auxiliary. At age 14 or 15 he began to suffer from psychiatric illness and underwent treatment at several south London hospitals. In November 1979, having been treated at the Adolescent Unit at Bexley Hospital for the previous 20 months, he was declared a 'management problem' because of his 'unpredictable, impulsive, uninhibited and violent' behaviour and was transferred to Broadmoor Hospital, where he was detained under the Mental Health Act 1959.

Broadmoor is a special hospital for the 'criminally insane' and for those who, although they have not committed any offence, are deemed to pose a danger if treated in an ordinary mental hospital. In reality, Broadmoor is run more as a prison than a hospital. This came as a shock to Michael Martin's mother when she first visited him there, since she had been told by the doctors who referred him only that he was being sent to another hospital to 'stabilise him'. Previously, at Bexley Hospital, he had been allowed home at weekends and went unaccompanied to clubs, sports centres and the church, without complaint from neighbours. At the hospital itself, he was allowed his own personal belongings – a radio, guitar, his own clothing. At Broadmoor, behind its high security fences, all this was denied to him.

Indeed, Martin continued to pose a 'management problem' at Broadmoor and, after a few months, he was transferred from the Young Persons' Unit at the hospital to the Special Care Unit at Norfolk House, which houses the most disturbed patients. During his time at Broadmoor, Martin was subjected to a range of treatments, including electroplexy and 'extensive trials' of various drugs to control his behaviour and 'to structure his encounters with other patients and members of the nursing staff.'[7] Yet, his mother claimed she was told

---

* The government has announced that Louis Blom-Cooper will head an inquiry into allegations of brutality at Ashworth top security hospital.[4] This followed the transmission of a 'Cutting Edge' programme in March 1991 entitled 'Special Hospital', in which former patients spoke of their experiences. In addition to allegations of brutality, a former patient decried the fact that prison officers had exhibited racism by bringing copies of *National Front News* into the wards (including those with black patients) and at least one serving officer sported a number of nazi-style tattoos.[5]

virtually nothing of his treatment. Initially, she visited her son, once or twice a week, despite the arduous journey from south London to Berkshire, but after a few months, around the time of Michael's transfer to Norfolk House, she was allegedly told she would no longer be allowed to come as her visits were 'upsetting' him. She says that nursing staff at the hospital refused to speak to her, hanging up the telephone when she called to enquire about Michael, and in the whole of the five years he was detained at Broadmoor, she saw his psychiatrist only once, he otherwise 'avoiding communication with her'.[8] She said that the psychiatrist only agreed to see her on that one occasion after she had threatened to take legal action over two black eyes Michael had suffered. She suspected that these were the result of his having been beaten, although the hospital claimed that they were self-inflicted, caused by Michael banging his head against a wall.

At that time, patients at Broadmoor considered Norfolk House to be something of a punishment block. It was divided into three wards, with the ground-floor Ward 1 for the 'most disturbed' patients. As a patient 'responded' to treatment, he would be transferred through Wards 2 and 3 on the next two floors, where there was slightly more freedom to move around, and eventually out of Norfolk House to other parts of the hospital. But if a patient became 'unmanageable', he could be transferred back to the more severe regime in Ward 1. The official inquiry held into Martin's death described conditions in Norfolk House at the time as 'conducive to boredom and frustration. In these circumstances outbursts of violence among patients were not altogether surprising.'[9] Only after Martin's death were improvements made so that, in the words of the inquiry report, patients could have 'access to fresh air and exercise' and, on Wards 2 and 3, be permitted free movement between the day room and dining room and to the toilets and even to attend church within the hospital.

At the time of his death, Michael Martin was one of 12 patients on Ward 3, and was under consideration for transfer out of Norfolk House (although his mother had not been told of this). Evidence given at his inquest indicates that he had been continuously subjected to racial abuse from another patient and that, despite his requests, staff had refused to intervene to stop this. The official inquiry report makes no mention of abuse from other patients, but instead attempts to dismiss allegations of racism on the basis of the inquiry's own interviews with staff, in which it is said that there was:

> no sign of racial prejudice. On the contrary the nursing staff at Norfolk House were particularly fond of [Martin] and he became something of a pet on the ward. The other patients tolerated him but found his behaviour, which was frequently childish and noisy, irritating . . . Mr Martin was short but very powerfully built.[10]

On the day of his death in July 1984, an argument broke out in the dayroom between Martin and the other patient and, after crossing the room to speak to the staff on duty and being told to sit down, Martin struck out at the other patient. There was then a struggle between Martin and a student nurse, during which another member of staff came up on Martin from the rear, grabbed him, and placed him in a headlock. All three men fell to the ground, with Martin continuing to be held around his neck. Another patient rang an alarm bell, which brought a 'swift' response from nursing staff all over the ward. Four of them picked Martin up and, as he allegedly continued to struggle, a fifth nurse placed him in another head hold with hands over both of his temples. He was taken to his room and undressed by six staff. At the inquest, another patient testified that he had heard a 'short, sharp, strangled cry' from the room, followed by silence.[11] It was then decided by the Ward 3 charge nurse that Martin should be given an injection of two major tranquillisers (known as a '5 and 2' injection), and orders for this were issued without consulting medical staff.

But before this injection could be administered, the charge nurse from Ward 1 arrived on the scene and proposed moving Martin immediately down the stairs to the ground floor. He was carried by six nurses, feet first and with his face downwards, down the two flights of stairs. On Ward 1 he was placed in a seclusion cell and held down as he was given the '5 and 2' injection, after which he was left lying in the cell, with his head towards the door, at 12.20pm. All the nurses from Ward 3 returned there, while the Ward 1 charge nurse called the hospital duty doctor (the Norfolk House doctor was on holiday at the time) and told him that Martin had been given an injection and was 'quiet and resting'. The doctor was not told that a struggle had taken place or that Martin had been injured, nor did he make any enquiries to this effect, simply telling the charge nurse that he would see Martin later that afternoon.

It is claimed that Martin was 'observed' periodically during the next 55 minutes, by five different members of staff, although no record was kept of any of these observations and the official inquiry confirmed that at least two of them consisted of no more than a quick glance, without any real check on Martin's condition. At 1.35pm, a nursing assistant realised that Martin had not changed his position since first being left in the cell, and he was found to be dead.

At the inquest, held in October 1984, another patient from Broadmoor testified that beatings and assaults on patients were a routine occurrence in Norfolk House. The post mortem on Martin revealed that he had died by choking on his own vomit, but it also showed that he had suffered extensive bruising to his body, probably from being removed down the stairs, and also to the front and sides of his neck, consistent with having been held in an armlock. The post mortem also suggested that the vomiting could have been caused by any of a number of factors, including excitement and high emotions associated with a violent struggle, a period of deprivation of oxygen caused by compression of the neck, and the administration of drugs. Equally, suppression of the gag reflex, which prevented the vomit from being expelled as normal, was attributed to either the injection of drugs or unconsciousness due to a lack of oxygen. The inquest jury returned a verdict of 'accidental death' aggravated by a lack of care.

As with so many of the deaths in police stations or prisons, the inquest into Michael Martin's death at Broadmoor, even with its 'lack of care' finding, might have resulted in no further official inquiries or actions. But Martin's family, supported by community groups and the prisoners' rights organisation, PROP, continued to protest and, with the support of a Labour MP, forced the Department of Health to establish an independent inquiry under Shirley Ritchie QC. The inquiry, which was held in private, concluded that the 'use of a neck hold [on Martin] was dangerous and should not have happened' and that it 'caused deep and extensive bruising and may have contributed to his vomiting and aspiration'; that he 'should not have been moved from Ward 3 to Ward 1 of Norfolk House at a time when he was still disturbed'; that the injection of drugs he received should not have been given without full consideration of 'his condition following a prolonged violent struggle'; that a doctor should have attended on Martin immediately and authorised any drugs to be administered to him; and that observation of Martin while in seclusion had been inadequate.[12]

The Ritchie inquiry concluded with a series of recommendations, among them that heavy sedative drugs should only be administered to patients on the specific instructions of a doctor in attendance at the time and that patients receiving such injections should then be placed under 'constant' observation. It was also proposed that all nursing staff should receive 'compulsory and regular' training in control and restraint techniques, according to guidelines specifying that 'talking and listening should be the first line of approach' to a disturbed patient and that the

> degree of force should be the minimum required to control the violence and it should be applied in a manner that attempts to reduce rather than provoke a further aggressive reaction. The number of staff involved should be the minimum necessary to restrain the patient while minimising injury to all parties.[13]

All bar one of these recommendations were officially accepted by the Department of Health, the one exception being that nursing staff were to continue to be allowed to administer sedatives to patients on the basis of 'advance' prescriptions from doctors.

However, two later cases where black men died in special hospitals throw the most serious doubts on the effectiveness of any changes introduced following Michael Martin's death. **Donald Chambers**[14] was

29 years old when, in September 1986, he died at Cane Hill Hospital in Coulsdon, Surrey, after being held down by nursing staff and given an injection. He died of what was termed Phentiazine Death Syndrome, which, as in the case of Michael Martin, involves the victim choking on his own vomit. There was also concern that Donald Chambers' family had never been properly informed about his being detained at the hospital under the Mental Health Act.

Just over four years after Michael Martin's death at Broadmoor, **Joseph Watts,**[15] aged 30, also died there, following an incident in which he was 'controlled and restrained' by a large group of nursing officers and was administered a heavy dose of sedative drugs. Watts was born in Kingston, Jamaica, in 1958 and came to England in 1970 to join his parents. At the age of 15 he received his first conviction, for theft, and four years later was convicted at Birmingham Crown Court of man-slaughter and received a five-year prison sentence. Following his release in 1980, he had a number of further, minor convictions and, in 1984, after being convicted of indecent assault, he was committed under the Mental Health Act to Broadmoor. At Broadmoor, Watts was not seen as presenting any 'management problems'. Instead, he was known as the 'gentle giant' because of his height (6 foot 3 inches) and weight (19-22 stone, although when admitted he weighed only 13 stone). He was also very religious, 'always reading the Bible', even though some of his nursing staff were later to deny any knowledge of his religious beliefs. In fact, like Richard Campbell and Harry Roberts (see below), Watts was a Rastafarian, and at one stage he complained that he had been refused permission to put up a poster of Haile Selassie and that staff had told him that if he didn't 'shut up about religion', he would be punished by having his medication increased. There were also some doubts about the diagnosis of Watts as schizophrenic, which had originally been made before his 1984 trial by a doctor at Brixton Prison but was challenged at the time by a senior lecturer in psychiatry at Atkinson Morley Hospital. These doubts about the diagnosis were reiterated in 1985 when Watts applied to a mental health review tribunal for release from Broadmoor, an application that was turned down. Before this, Watts had also complained that he had been sexually assaulted by a member of the hospital's nursing staff.

In April 1986, Watts was recorded as having lost 'privileges' as a result of 'unspecified inappropriate conduct towards female staff'.[16] But the following July, he was allowed to join a team of patients doing bricklaying work at the hospital and, by October 1986, he had made sufficient improvement to be moved to a ward catering for 'lower dependency needs' patients. In March 1987, it was recorded that he had been attending 'mixed socials' for three months and was progressing well. But, in November of that year, he was again observed 'behaving inappropriately' in the presence of female staff. This behaviour was said to consist of his 'staring intently . . . beliefs and recent behaviour suggest recurrence of paranoid psychosis'.[17] As a result, he was returned to a more restrictive ward and his medication was increased – at one stage, it was even considered moving him to Norfolk House where Michael Martin had died in 1984. His doctor at this time admitted at a subsequent inquiry into Watts' death that his behaviour may have been due to physical rather than mental causes, stemming from an injury to his brain.

From this point in late 1987 to his death in August 1988, Joseph Watts' conditions of life inside Broadmoor sharply deteriorated. His medication was further increased in January 1988, when his complaints of homosexual advances from other patients were dismissed as delusional. In March of that year, he was transferred to the care of a locum psychiatrist, who, as the inquiry into Watts' death noted, had 'made no record of her interviews with and examinations of Mr Watts' from then on. In July 1988, his activities at the hospital were 'severely curtailed', as his placement on the bricklaying team was withdrawn (again supposedly because of possible contact with female staff) and no other steps were taken to occupy his time or to provide him with physical exercise. One nursing staff member described him as 'lazy', but the inquiry following his death concluded that 'there was little if any consideration of the effects of being confined to [the ward] upon Mr Watts'.[18] At about this time, Watts told his solicitor, then preparing for a further appeal to a mental health review tribunal, that 'my life is in danger'.[19] The tribunal hearing was postponed, and the next month, before it could be reconvened, Joseph Watts was dead.

He died on the evening of 28 August, following an incident which started, as in the case of Michael Martin, in an argument with another patient, in this case in the dormitory of his ward inside Kent House. An alarm bell in the dormitory was pushed by another patient, which in ordinary circumstances would have led to between 10 and 12 staff responding. In this instance, however, according to some witnesses, as many as 60 staff finally entered the ward. In the meantime, a group of staff entered the dormitory and separated Watts and the other patient. It was then decided, as a matter of routine procedure and without any attempt to 'talk and listen' to either patient or discover the causes of their argument, to remove them both, using 'control and restraint' techniques, and to isolate them in separate rooms.

The inquiry into Watts' death stated that the accounts conflicted about how he responded to being relocated in this way, with some nursing staff saying that he went calmly and others claiming that he had been 'verbally aggressive'. However, while the patients were being moved, very large numbers of hospital staff were still rushing into the ward from other parts of the hospital and occupying the corridor along which patients were being taken. As the inquiry concluded: 'It is by no means clear to us that, given the nature of events then and subsequently, especially the arrival on the ward of such numbers of nursing staff, that [the charge nurse] would effectively have been able to manage the situation. In particular, we have received no convincing evidence to suggest that anyone took steps to ensure that the number of staff remaining on the ward was commensurate with the number necessary to contain the situation.'[20]

Once Watts had reached the seclusion room, what the inquiry called 'a physically violent altercation' took place between him and 'an indeterminate number of nursing staff'.[21] Eventually, all the staff left the room and locked the door behind them. But it was then observed that Watts had with him a damaged pair of spectacles and the spectacles' case belonging to one of the nursing staff. A decision was made to re-enter the room, this time with staff fitted out with riot helmets and shields, in order to 'disarm' him and to administer a major dose of intra-muscular tranquilliser to him. Volunteers were requested from among the staff present who had received the proper training in 'control and restraint' techniques, but it then emerged that no staff at Broadmoor had been given such training (which was supposedly made 'compulsory and routine' in 1985 following the inquiry into Michael Martin's death) during the previous 21 months.

The nurse in charge claimed at the subsequent inquiry that no more than five staff entered Watts' room the second time and that they successfully restrained him 'with difficulty'. But another nurse involved told the police only two days after the incident that extra staff had had to be called and that 10 in all restrained Watts by struggling with him. The inquiry team itself reported that it was 'unable confidently to conclude' that the conflict of evidence it had received arose 'from a natural and understandable difference of impression of events gained by those who were witness to the facts'.[22] Nor was the inquiry able to comment on the suitability of the heavy dose of tranquilliser given to Watts, while he was being held down by a large group of nursing staff. After this, he was left alone in the room, with no specific instructions given as to who would be responsible for observing him. Two minutes later, he was seen to have stopped breathing and was found to be dead.

Harry Roberts,[23] otherwise known as **Rush I**, was another Rastafarian to die in a special hospital, in this case a unit at Prestwich Hospital in Cheshire, where he was found hanged in March 1985. While serving an earlier prison sentence, from which he was released in 1982, Rush I had developed a close interest in Africa and ties with other black prisoners, to whom he was known for his 'natural resistance' to the harassment he received, as a Rastafarian, in prison. He was arrested in 1984 for stabbing a policeman, and was remanded for eight months to Strangeways Prison in Manchester. In accordance with his principles as a Rastafarian, he eventually refused to enter a plea or recognise the court and, as a result, he was referred by the magistrates to Prestwich for observation. Two weeks later, he was found dead in the security wing of the hospital. One of the black prisoners who had known Rush I later wrote, 'I can believe he refused to recognise the court – it's an act of defiance he was well capable of. But I could never imagine his committing suicide. He had too much rebel spirit, too much pride, too many ambitions and too many dreams to fulfil to do anything like that.'[24]

CHAPTER 4

Roll call of deaths

We list below those deaths of black people which have taken place in prison, police or hospital custody and which have given rise to concern because of unexplained or mysterious circumstances surrounding those deaths, and/or allegations of maltreatment, dereliction of duty or brutality.

We have tried, wherever possible, to give more than one source for each case. But it is inevitable that, given the closed nature of the institutions and lack of accountability, we can on occasion give only one source of information. For it is non-mainstream black papers like Black Voice *and* Voice *which make it their particular business to bring to light cases which the rest of the media ignore. Far from being written off as alarmist or partial, they should be commended for the service they render. Where information has been provided by lawyers from inquests or from the organisation Inquest, it has been indicated.*

We have tried to give the inquest verdicts (IV) reached on the deaths of each person. Unfortunately, that information has not always been available.

1969

18 April: **David Oluwale**, 38, vagrant. Body was found in River Aire, Leeds. IV: *found drowned.* Two policemen subsequently found guilty of assaulting him. ('The death of one lame darkie', *Race Today,* January 1973; Jeremy Seabrook, *Smiling David,* London, Calder and Boyars, 1974)

1971

29 April: **Andre Savvas**. Died from a fractured skull in Hornsey police station. (*Black Voice,* Vol. 3, no. 1)

13 May: **Aseta Simms**, housewife. Died in Stoke Newington police station. IV: *death by misadventure,* unexplained bruising found on body. (*Black Voice,* Vol. 2, no. 4; Melissa Benn and Ken Worpole, *Death in the City,* London, Canary Press, 1986)

1972

Lil' Douza, 17. Died in Oxford detention centre. IV: *pneumonia virus.*

The jaw was swollen and there was blood around nose and mouth. (*Black Voice*, Vol. 3, no. 2)

1973

26 November: **Horace Bailey**. Died from hanging in Ashford Remand Centre. IV: *suicide*. He had been awaiting trial for three months and was in obvious need of psychiatric care. He hanged himself on the day that the prison doctor had finally decided he should be moved to a mental hospital. (*West Indian World*, 4.1.74)

1974

5 February: **Stephen Bernard**, 33, law student. Died 15 hours after being released from Ladywell police station. IV: *acute bronchitis*. His relatives demanded a public inquiry to find out why Stephen had been taken to a police station when they had asked for an ambulance to take him to Bexley Hospital (where he was known as a psychiatric patient), what happened there, and how he developed acute bronchitis when he had no bronchial history. (*Black Voice*, Vol. 5, no. 2; *West Indian World*, 22.5.74; *Race Today*, June 1974)

20 February: **Joseph Lawrence**. Died in Brixton prison. IV: *natural causes*. 11 Brixton prisoners smuggled out a letter stating he had been beaten up at the prison. (*Black Voice*, Vol. 5, no. 2)

26 May: **John Lamaletie**. Died of a bloodclot in an artery leading to the brain nine days after his neck had been restricted by police (and his artery kinked) and he had allegedly been severely beaten in Hornsey police station. IV: *accidental death*. The coroner, Dr Davies, told the jury that he would leave out of the record its rider 'while under police restraint'. (*Black Voice*, Vol. 5, no. 3)

1977

17 January: **Adeenarain Neelayya**, 32, nurse. Taken to Chatham police station after a traffic accident, suspected of being drunk or drugged. He was dead in the cell within one hour. (*West Indian World*, 4.2.1977)

9 November: **Basil Brown**, 25. Died in Albany Prison. Family say they were prevented from removing covers over the body and were not told why bruises and cuts were visible. (*Grassroots*, March-April 1978)

1978

10 December: **Michael Ferreira**, 19. Died after being interrogated by

Stoke Newington police. He had been stabbed by racist youths (who were later convicted of manslaughter), but police were criticised for questioning him rather than getting help. (*Death in the City*, op. cit.; *Grassroots*, Feb-March 1979)

1979

2 August: **S. Singh Grewal**, 40. Was taken to Southall police station and died of inhalation of vomit. His family and doctor were not allowed to see the body for nine days. (*The fight against racism*, London, IRR, 1986)

23 August: **Henry Floyd**, 26. Found hanged in cell of West End Central police station, after arrest in London shop. IV: *suicide*. He was seen to be hit whilst being arrested. (*West Indian World*, 16.11.79)

24 October: **John Eshiett**, 26. Died in Brixton Prison whilst awaiting trial. (*West Indian World*, 16.11.79)

1980

31 March: **Richard Campbell**, 19. Died of dehydration in Ashford Remand Centre after being given large quantities of drugs and being force-fed. IV: *death by self-neglect with rider on inadequate medical facilities*. Jury not allowed to bring in a verdict blaming the authorities. Family appeal against the inquest verdict in High Court. Independent enquiry convened by Battersea and Wandsworth Trades Council. (*West Indian World*, 11.4.80, 18.7.80; *New Statesman*, 4.7.80; *The death of Richard 'Cartoon' Campbell*, London, Battersea and Wandsworth Trades Council, 1981)

August: **Leroy Gordon**, 20. Died in Pershore police station, Birmingham, after a crowd, suspecting him of a robbery, had sat on him. IV: *death by asphyxiation due to compression of neck*. (*CARF/Searchlight*, October 1980)

1981

13 July: **Winston Rose**, 27, electrician. Died in a police van whilst being forcibly restrained on the way to psychiatric hospital. IV: *unlawful killing at the hands of the police*. In 1990 his family was awarded £130,000 damages, but no apology came from the police and no one was prosecuted for the death. (*Black Voice*, Vol. 12, no. 3; *CARF/Searchlight*, Sept, Dec, 1981, April 1990; *Caribbean Times*, 13.2.90)

6 November: **Shohik Meah**, 43. Died in a cell at Thornhill Road police station, Birmingham, following his arrest. It was alleged that he had an epileptic fit followed by a heart attack, but he also had a fractured nose and bruising. (*Black Voice*, Vol. 12, no. 3; *Caribbean Times*, 13.11.81)

1982

12 January: **Paul Worrell**, 21, amateur boxer. He was found hanged in Brixton Prison. IV: *open verdict.* Community defence campaign launched to ask why, though mentally ill, he was remanded in prison; why, though a suicide risk, he was allowed materials which enabled him to hang himself. (*Kentish Independent*, 14.10.82; *Evening Standard*, 8.3.83; *Brixton Defence Campaign Bulletin*, No. 4)

25 March: **Singh Changa**, 60. Died in Cathays Park police station, Bristol. IV: *misadventure.* Family asked why, when he had acute alcohol poisoning, he was not taken to hospital. (*South Wales Echo*, 14.10.82; *Bristol Evening Post*, 15.10.82)

September 1982; **Franklyn Lee**, 20. Died, according to police, of injuries sustained during a burglary. But witnesses allege he was dragged 70 yards down the road to a police van and there was a delay in calling an ambulance. (*West Indian World*, 10.9.82; *Brixton Defence Campaign Bulletin*, No 6)

10 December: **Simeon Collins**. 17, student. He was arrested by City Road police for being 'drunk and incapable'; following day died in hospital of injuries to liver and spleen. IV: *accidental death.* Family asked for inquest to be re-opened because so much evidence conflicted and questions were left unanswered. (Inquest; *Militant*, 19.8.83)

1983

12 January: **Colin Roach**. Died of shot-gun blast in Stoke Newington police station. IV: *suicide.* Jury writes to Home Office about police insensitivity; family, community groups and Independent Enquiry Into Policing in Hackney 1945-85 demand further inquiry into death. (*CARF/Searchlight*, August 1983, January 1984; *Caribbean Times* 11.2.83, 24.6.83, 17.2.84; *Inquest Bulletin*, No. 7, 1985; *Voice*, 19.1.1988; *Hackney Gazette*, 15.1.88)

14 February: **James Ruddock**, 44, suffered from diabetes and sickle cell anaemia. Died from hypothermia in St Stephens' Hospital after being kept without treatment for 12 hours in Kensington police station. IV: *natural causes attributed (sic) by self-neglect.* (Inquest; *Kensington News and Post*, 31.3.83; *Daily Telegraph*, 24.3.83; *Morning Star*, 24.3.83)

6 May: **Matthew Paul**, 19. Hanged himself in Leman police station. IV: *suicide due to lack of care.* Jurors criticised the cell conditions and fact that wicket gate was left open on cell door. He had been held as a murder suspect for 36 hours without access to his mother or a lawyer. The inquest was delayed until after the murder trial, by which time the body, which had not been kept in a deep freeze, had deteriorated. (Inquest; *East London Advertiser*, 13.5.83; *Newham Recorder*, 15/18.12.83; *Hackney Gazette*, 9.12.83; *Inquest Bulletin*, No. 1, Dec 1983; *Daily Mail*, 7.5.83)

5 May: **Nicholas Ofusu**, 31. Suffering psychiatric disorder, choked on his own vomit after Rotherhithe police allegedly handcuffed him, bundled him into a van and kept him on the floor. IV: *death by misadventure*. (*Death in the city*, op. cit.; *Daily Telegraph*, 12.7.83; *South East London Mercury*, 19.5.83; *Evening Standard*, 15.5.83; *Guardian*, 16.7.83; *South London Press*, 20.5.83; *Scotsman*, 16.7.83)

6 December: **Leslie George Hoo Singh**. Fell from 4th floor window of Hammersmith Hospital where he had been transferred from Wormwood Scrubs Prison. (*Morning Star*, 5.1.84)

1984

6 July: **Michael Dean Martin**, 22. Choked on his own vomit after being injected with a tranquilliser drug. IV: *accidental death aggravated by lack of care*. An inquiry was held by the Department of Health and Social Security which made new recommendations about the treatment of patients. (*South London Press*, 21.3.86; *CARF/Searchlight* June 1985; *Glasgow Herald*, 2.9.85; *Daily Telegraph*, 31.8.85; *Guardian*, 19.7.86; *Open Mind*, Feb/March 1985)

21 October: **Curtis Marsh**, 27, dustman. Hanged himself in Brixton Prison. IV: *suicide*. Though the authorities had been warned of his suicidal tendencies, he was alone in an ordinary cell and, like 10 others in Brixton who hanged themselves in 1983 and 1984, he was on 'special watch B'. (*Caribbean Times*, 11.1.85; *Hornsey Journal*, 9.11.84)

1985

2 January: **Chittaranjan Pragalee Joshi**. Found hanged in Pentonville Prison whilst on remand. IV: *suicide*. He intended to appeal against extradition to the USA. (*Caribbean Times*, 11.1.85; *Abolitionist*, No. 2, 1985)

11 March: **Harold Roberts [Rush I]**. Found hanged in secure unit of Prestwich Hospital. IV: *suicide*. He had waited for eight months on remand in Strangeways, had refused to recognise the court or enter a plea and two days before death had been restrained and drugged. (*Inquest Bulletin*, No. 7, 1985; 'Letter from prisoner', *CARF/*

Searchlight, August 1985)

30 March: **James Hall**. Psychiatric patient died in Lavender Hill police station. IV: *misadventure*. Police believed he was drunk, whereas he had overdosed on drugs and had a ruptured spleen. (*Standard*, 23.5.85; *South London Press*, 7.11.86)

15 July: **John Mikkelson**, 34. Died by asphyxiating on his own vomit at Hounslow police station after being forcibly restrained by police, hit on head, bundled into van and allegedly left on charge-room floor. IV: *unlawful killing*. Second inquest ordered after appeal by police to High Court. IV: *misadventure*. Seven officers were suspended but not charged. (*Abolitionist*, Nos 21, 22, 1986; *Policing London*, Sept/Oct 1986; *Observer*, 21.12.86; *Voice*, 15.11.86, 21.12.86, 28.3.87; *Guardian*, 4.11.86, 20.12.86, 20.2.87, 20.5.87; *Independent*, 1.2.87; *Times*, 9.4.87)

6 October: **Cynthia Jarrett**. Died of a heart attack during a raid on her Tottenham home. IV: *accidental death*. (*Guardian*, 30.1.85, 2.12.85, 14.12.85; *Race Today*, January 1986)

1986

Keith Hicks, 34, an epileptic and schizophrenic. Died in a Brixton prison cell one day before he was due to be moved to a special hospital. IV: *misadventure*. Family protested that they could not get details of death from Prison Department. (*Independent*, 24.12.86)

12 August: **Stephen Bogle**, 27, shoe-maker. Died of sickle-cell anaemia in cells of Thames Magistrates' Court. IV: *natural causes aggravated by lack of care*. His condition was never diagnosed or treated during one week in custody. He was left lying on floor of cell at court. (*Voice*, 31.1.87; *Guardian*, 20.1.87)

11 September: **Donald Paul Chambers**, 29. Choked to death on his own vomit at Cane Hill Hospital, Surrey. IV: *death by misadventure*. The inquest ruled he died from Phentiazine Death Syndrome, which causes victims to choke on their vomit. He had been forcibly held down and injected by nurses just prior to his death. Mother angry that she did not know he was detained under the Mental Health Act and questions inquest verdict. (Inquest; *Voice*, 24.1.87)

6 October: **M. Anwar Kureshi**. Hanged himself in Brixton Prison. IV: *suicide*. He had been on remand for 10 months charged with conspiracy and buggery with a 16-year-old. Charges had been changed but he was not informed. Though on special watch he was in a normal cell despite a previous suicide attempt. (*Guardian*, 8.1.87)

8 October: **Caiphas Anthony Lemard**. Died in Kensington police station choking on his own vomit. IV: *non-dependent drug abuse aggravated by lack of care*. Witnesses said they saw him being man-handled in the police van. Community groups angry that police put out press reports that he had used a huge dose of cocaine. Three post-mortems held. Police Complaints authority investigated and concluded that no charges should be brought against police involved. (*Guardian*, 10.10.86, 11.10.86, 5.11.86, 20.10.86; *Standard*, 4.11.86, 17.10.86, 9.10.86; *Willesden and Brent Chronicle*, 24.10.86; *Police Complaints Authority News Release*, 5.2.87; *Police Review*, 14.11.86; *Daily Telegraph*, 27.12.86)

1987

27 January: **Akhtar Moghul**, 47. Died in Holloway Prison. IV: *death by natural causes aggravated by lack of care*. Held on remand accused of smuggling heroin from Pakistan. Spoke no English and was allegedly denied medical care despite a heart condition. (*Abolitionist*, No. 23, 1987; *Asian Times*, 20.2.87, *Asian Women in Prison Group Press Release*)

20 February: **Clinton McCurbin**. Choked to death during a struggle with police in Next shop, Wolverhampton. IV: *death by misadventure*. Witnesses said that the police had used undue force in a neck-hold; police issued a statement that the death was related to drug abuse. The Police Complaints Authority decided that the two officers involved should not be prosecuted. (*Birmingham Evening Mail*, 21.2.87, 23.2.87; *Observer*, 22.2.87, *Independent*, 27.2.87, 22.8.87, 2.11.88; *Wolverhampton Council for Community Relations*, *Voice*, 28.2.87, 7.3.87, 25.8.87, 20.12.88)

23 March: **Ahmed Katangole**, 24. Found hanged in cell in Pentonville Prison. IV: *suicide aggravated by official indifference and lack of care*. He was due to be removed to Uganda after being twice refused political asylum. Had attempted suicide before and should have been more closely observed, according to the British Refugee Council, which also called for a Home Office inquiry. (*CARF/Searchlight*, August 1987; *Newham Recorder*, 2.4.87; *Voice*, 7.7.87; Inquest; *Guardian*, 3.7.87)

23 April: **Rai Jasbir Singh**, 32. Found hanged in Wakefield Prison. (*Morning Star*, 25.4.87)

24 April: **Nenneh Jalloh**. Fell to her death from 4th floor window of Marylebone police station while being held on shop-lifting charge. IV: *death by misadventure*. (*Asian Times*, 29.5.87; *Observer*, 3.5.87; *News on Sunday*, 28.6.87)

1 May: **Mohammed Parkit**, 50, restaurant worker. Died of cardiac arrest 24 hours after being taken in for questioning at Marylebone police station. IV: *open verdict*. (*Asian Times*, 29.5.87; *Seven Days*, 4.7.87)

18 May: **Anachu Anozie Osita**, 28. Died in a prison van transferring him from Wormwood Scrubs to Brixton for medical treatment. IV: *natural causes aggravated by lack of care.* Staff had used a restraining body belt on him without the governor's permission. (*Guardian*, 23.5.87; *Shepherds Bush & Hammersmith Gazette*, 10.7.87)

26 June: **Tunay Hassan**, 25. Died in Dalston police station. IV: *drug dependency aggravated by lack of care.* His girlfriend, who was taken in for questioning with him, said he had been severely beaten by police; she killed herself 48 hours later. Family asked for second post mortem. Body badly deteriorated because refrigeration had failed. Community call for public inquiry. (*Hackney Gazette*, 3.7.87, 4.12.87; *Guardian*, 27.6.87, 15.1.88, 23.1.88; *City Limits*, 10.12.87)

August: **Terence Brown**, 35, youth worker. Died in Tooting Bec hospital. IV: *open verdict*, He was allegedly drugged, locked in a bare room for three hours and there choked on his own vomit. (*Voice*, 5.1.88, 16.2.88)

19 August: **Anthony Mahony**, 24, painter. Died, with almost no clothes on, of pneumonia in a strip cell at Brixton Prison. IV: *natural causes aggravated by lack of care.* Despite a history of mental illness, he was sent to Brixton when suspected of indecent exposure. Viral pneumonia was not diagnosed. (*Voice*, 16.2.88; *Inquest Bulletin*, No. 10, 1987)

24 September: **Mark Ventour**. Found drowned in River Nene, Northampton, two weeks after family reported him missing. IV: *asphyxia caused by chewing gum in throat.* Family, who had been told by a friend that son had been taken into custody, called for independent autopsy – which showed bruising on body and that the ankles had been tied. (*Northampton Post*, 16.10.87; *Voice*, 20.10.87; *Caribbean Times*, 23.10.87, 27.11.87)

October 1987: **Joseph Palombella**, 40. Found dead in cell at Belle Vale police station, Liverpool. (*Guardian*, 17.11.87)

1988

5 February: **Samuel Carew**, 22. Killed himself in Brixton Prison hospital wing. IV: *suicide.* Coroner asked for psychiatric assessments to be speeded up. Carew had been remanded for nearly two weeks for medical reports. (*Voice*. 11.6.89; Inquest)

February: **Femi Adelaja**, 36. Died of a heart condition in a cell at Old Bailey. A founder of Croydon Black Peoples' Action Committee which monitored police racism. He and others were on a £200,000 fraud charge; while held on remand for 10 months, he was denied treatment for sarcoidosis of the heart. (*Time Out*, 29.6.88)

16 March: **Armando Belonia.** Died of pneumonia in a locked ward of hospital wing of Wandsworth Prison. IV: *death by natural causes aggravated by lack of care.* Coroner reported the matter to the Board of Visitors' because the victim had been given pain-killers for back-ache and never examined properly; the pain-killers were, in fact, potentially lethal to someone suffering from pneumonia. Prison doctor was struck off. (*Guardian*, 25.6.88, 25.7.90; *Board of Visitors Inquiry*)

13 May: **Bahader Singh**, 26. Died in India hours after arriving from Barlinnie jail, where he had suffered physical and racial abuse. (*Asian Times*, 24.8.88; *Abolitionist*, No. 16, 1988)

June 1988: **Oakley Ramsey**, 25. Suffocated by inhaling vomit following a disturbance in which he was sat upon by another man and police arrived to arrest him and put him in hand-cuffs. Family demanded independent post mortem and inquiry. (*Caribbean Times*, 10.6.88, 17.6.88; *Voice*, 14.6.88)

20 June: **Kelroy Briscoe**, 32, hospital worker. Hanged himself in Wormwood Scrubs Prison. He was due to be bailed on a domestic violence charge. (*Willesden and Brent Chronicle*, 30.6.88)

23 August: **Joseph Watts**, 30. Died in Broadmoor. IV: *accidental death.* Sedated by dose of tranquilliser drug following a scuffle. Family tried to get public inquiry. (*Voice*, 29.11.88, 24.1.89 *Special Hospitals Service Authority Inquiry*, July 1989)

4 September: **Sajjan Singh Atwal**, 36. Hanged himself in Winson Green Prison. IV: *lack of care.* Verdict quashed; second verdict: *suicide due to lack of care.* He had already made a suicide attempt a week earlier and was refusing food. He was last seen at 9pm on 3.9.88. (Inquest; *Eastern Eye*, 13.11.90; *Derby Evening Telegraph*, 27.10.90; *Guardian*, 25.10.90)

4 September: **Derek Stephen Buchanan**, 19. Found drowned in River Colne, Huddersfield. IV: *drowning.* Family suspicious because died after police chase and he was a good swimmer. (*Caribbean Times*, 30.9.88, 29.10.88, 14.4.89; *Voice*, 25.4.89)

4 December: **Martin Richmond**, 30. Found hanged in Brixton Prison. IV: *open verdict.* Family asked why officers did not find son's body earlier and why he killed himself when he had no history of depression. (*Caribbean Times*, 13.1.89; *Voice*, 14.3.89)

December: **Wayne Tombison.** Found hanged in cell in Maidstone Prison, Kent. Parents angry that the authorities had failed to note son's history of psychiatric disorder and had given him a single cell. (*Voice*, 6.12.88)

1989

22 February: **David 'Duke' Daley**, 24, gardener. Found hanged with own jumper in cell at Marylebone Magistrates's Court. IV: *open verdict.* A private post mortem cast doubts on the hanging and suggested that an arm-lock could have been used on him prior to death.(*Voice*, 14.3.89, 18.4.89; *Time Out*, 17.5.89)

March 1989: **Nicholas Bramble**, 17. Killed when motorbike hit lamp-post. IV: *accidental death.* He was allegedly being chased by seven police cars when death happened. Community groups staged protests. (*Voice*, 20.6.89, 11.4.89, 13.3.90)

July 1989: **Vincent Graham**, 40, dress cutter. Police alleged that he stabbed himself as he was pursued in City Road, London, after they tried to question him. (*Caribbean Times*, 21.7.89; *Voice*, 8.8.89)

2 July: **Jamie Stewart**, 22. Died in cell of Holloway Road police station. IV: *death by misadventure due to an excessive overdose of cocaine.* Arrested on suspicion of driving a stolen car, restrained, handcuffed and locked in a cell. (*Caribbean Times*, 14.7.89, 22.7.89, 28.7.89; *Legal Action*, October 1989; *Voice*, 11.7.89; *City Limits*, 8.2.90; *Guardian*, 3.7.89)

12 July: **Edwin Carr**, 39, salesman. Died in King's College Hospital after being on life-support machine. He had been taken to Carter Street police station because police found a small quantity of cannabis on him. Previously in good health (though on crutches because of a weak knee), hours later, he collapsed and was rushed to hospital. (*Voice*, 12.7.89; *Caribbean Times*, 14.7.89)

October 1989: **Mr Romany**. Found dead in Chanings Wood Prison, Devon. Other prisoners stated that his screaming for a day and a night had been ignored. (*Voice*, 14.11.89)

5 October: **Siho Iyugiven**, 27, Kurdish refugee from Turkey. Died from burns at Harmondsworth Detention Centre. IV: *misadventure.* He had been denied political asylum and detained at Harmondsworth pending removal. He and cell-mate went on hunger strike, barricaded themselves in room and set bedding alight as a protest; smoke detectors were not working, few fire extinguishers worked, building had no sprinklers. (Inquest)

6 December: **Germain Alexander**, 58. Died in Brixton Prison. IV: *death by natural causes aggravated by lack of care.* Died hours after being admitted; post mortem showed bruising all over body, broken teeth in mouth and fractured spine. Coroner called for urgent review of psychiatric care in prisons as no one had been able to deal medically with his 'manic' state; instead, 'control and restraint' techniques involving shields and helmets had been used to move him to strip cell. Family considering bringing civil action for negligence against Home Office Prison Medical Service. (*Voice*, 2.1.90; *Time Out*, 20.12.89; *Caribbean Times*, 6.12.89; *Independent*, 13.4.90; *Caribbean Times*, 17.4.90; *Guardian*, 13.4.90)

1990

15 June: **Kimpua Nsimba**, 24. Found hanged in Harmondsworth Detention Centre. IV: *suicide*. Came from Zaire claiming asylum. No one spoke to him in Harmondsworth for four days; body not found for over 20 hours. The private security firm which runs the centre, had no training in suicide prevention. (*Guardian*, 6.3.91; Inquest)

July: **Oliver Pryce**, 30. Arrested by five Middlesborough police officers, collapsed in police van, taken to hospital where pronounced dead. Family blamed police for the death. An independent medical examination concluded that he died of asphyxiation. Police report has been sent to DPP. (*Voice*, 7.8.90, 22.1.91)

12 October: **Aslam Khan**, 29. Hanged himself in Brixton Prison whilst on remand. (*Time Out*, 7.11.90)

30 November: **Edwin Robinson**, 28. Hanged himself in Brixton Prison. IV: *killed himself because of lack of care.* He had been diagnosed as suffering from a psychotic illness, but social workers did not appear in court so that he could be sent to hospital under section 2 of the Mental Health Act. When nurses did come to court and agreed to his suitability for medical care, no bed could be found, so he was sent back to Brixton medical wing where he saw no doctor and staff were not aware he was a suicide risk. Coroner made five recommendations about the urgent need for better communications between courts and prisons and all prison staff about medical care. (*Guardian*, 4, 6.4.91)

1991

19 January: **Delroy McKnight**, 29, labourer. Cut his own throat with a piece of cell window glass and bled to death at Wandsworth Prison. IV: *killed himself while the balance of mind was disturbed and the cause of death was contributed to by lack of care.* Though diagnosed as suffering from acute paranoid schizophrenia, he was never examined by a psychiatrist during his 10 months in prison and, though a suicide risk, was not on special watch when transferred from High Point to Wandsworth in December 1990. Coroner made recommendations about medical care and suicide prevention. (*Time Out*, 6.2.91; *Guardian*, 8.3.91; Inquest)

CHAPTER 5

Recommendations

As we have been preparing this book, the issue of deaths in custody, particularly in prisons, has gained increasing public notice, not least through the reports of Her Majesty's Chief Inspector of Prisons, Judge Stephen Tumim,[1] and the public condemnations by coroners following inquests into a number of recent deaths.[2] But it certainly has not always been the case that deaths in custody, especially those of black people, have been the subject of so much official and media attention. Too often, the organs of the state and the established press have served instead to obscure and cover up the facts about black people dying at the hands of the police and in prison and hospital custody. In these circumstances, it has only been through the campaigns of black families and communities, the black press and organisations such as Inquest that the truth about so many deaths in custody has come to light.

The black community's experience on this issue mirrors exactly what it has known in respect of racial attacks in general – years of official indifference and even hostility towards those trying to expose the truth in individual cases. And, just as the black community has learned that its first, and often only, line of defence against racial violence lies in the actions of black people themselves, so any recommendations for reform in relation to black people dying in custody must begin with steps to protect and assert the basic human rights of black people as individuals, as families, and as communities.

Keeping black people out of custody

The first of the rights that must be asserted is that of equal treatment before the law, for if there were not so many black people ensnared within the criminal justice system, far fewer of them would end up dying in custody. There is now an overwhelming body of evidence to demonstrate that black people suffer unequal treatment at every stage of the criminal legal process – from the over-policing of black communities and events and the massively disproportionate stopping, searching and arresting of black people; to their being denied bail, charged (rather than cautioned), convicted (or sectioned under the Mental Health Acts) and given custodial sentences far more frequently than white people; to their being held for much longer periods in various form of custody (see Appendix). Over 10 years ago, we compiled our first body of evidence on the unequal treatment of black people before the forces of the criminal law, to be presented to the then Royal Commission on Criminal Procedure.[3] Unfortunately, the report that eventually emerged from that Royal Commission virtually ignored, as had the Scarman Report before it, the racist dimensions of policing and law enforcement in Britain. Now, as we write, a new Royal Commission on Criminal Justice is about to embark on its work, again without any specific remit to tackle issues of racism in what, for black people, is so often a system of criminal injustice. Our first recommendation, therefore, is that the Royal Commission on Criminal Justice must make the unequal treatment of black people and the widescale denial of their rights at every stage in the criminal legal process one of its central concerns.

But there are immediate steps that must be taken as well to keep more black people out of custody. The evidence shows that black people face a particular problem in terms of remands for medical and psychiatric reports and commitals to prison or hospital custody under the Mental Health Acts. As Judge Stephen Tumim has noted in one of his recent reports, excessive numbers of remands in custody for these purposes 'represent a serious infringement of personal liberty, especially when some of those remanded in custody have been charged with non-imprisonable offences'.[4] His report goes on to commend the setting up of duty psychiatric schemes to provide on-the-spot assessments of defendants at magistrates' courts, and the evidence from the few schemes which operate at present does show that they can result in many more defendants being released immediately and the diversion of others to hospitals without the necessity of their spending any time in prison.

But, as shown in the case of Edwin Robinson, who was remanded to Brixton Prison from a court with a duty psychiatric scheme and later committed suicide, such schemes are only as effective as the back-up services available to them. In the Robinson case, no social worker could be found to attend court to confirm the duty psychiatrist's assessment, nor was any bed immediately available for him in local hospitals.[5] There is a need, in particular, to provide alternatives to both prison and hospital custody for the non-dangerous mentally ill, whether in the form of structured bail hostels with psychiatric support or community-based facilities for the assessment and longer term treatment of such persons. And, given the continuing failures of the mental health system in this country to provide proper assessment and appropriate treatment for so many black people diagnosed as schizophrenic, the need for community treatment facilities directly involving black mental health groups is particularly acute.

In the meantime, the provisions of the Bail Act must be urgently reviewed so as to provide specific safeguards for unconvicted persons against being remanded in custody for medical or psychiatric reports. Such remands should be barred where the defendant is charged with a non-imprisonable offence and otherwise only allowed where the court can show that all possible alternatives have been considered. And where such remands in custody for reports do take place, they should be subject to strict time limits of no more than two or three days.

Another group of black prisoners who should be diverted out of custody altogether are those seeking asylum. It is particularly inhumane that those who arrive in this country under extreme duress, often having escaped from torture and oppressive treatment abroad, should be immediately locked up and held for long periods while their applications for asylum are considered. Indeed, precisely because of their political and social isolation and the fears they have of being unjustly denied refuge and forcibly returned to their countries of origin, asylum-seekers are known to be particularly vulnerable to suicide. There should be an absolute bar on the detention of asylum-seekers who should in every case be granted temporary admission while their applications are considered.

• **The Royal Commission on Criminal Justice should give special consideration to racism and the unequal treatment of black people in the criminal justice system.**

• **Duty psychiatric schemes, properly backed-up by other professional services, should be available at all magistrates' courts.**

• **The Bail Act should be urgently reviewed to provide tight limitations on the right of courts to remand unconvicted persons in custody for reports and stricter time-limits for such remands where they do take place.**

• **More resources need to be provided for bail hostels and community-based treatment facilities for the assessment and treatment of the non-dangerous mentally ill, involving, where appropriate, black community mental health groups.**

• **The detention of asylum-seekers should be abolished and, in every case, they should be granted temporary admission while awaiting decisions on their applications**

Protecting the rights of black people in custody

Recently, a great deal of attention has been focused on the need to take positive measures to prevent deaths in prison. Indeed, the recent Tumim Report on *Suicide and Self-Harm in Prison Service Establishments*[6] contains no less than 123 recommendations for change, while bodies such as Inquest and the National Association of Probation Officers (NAPO) have gone further and called for the abolition of the Prison Medical Service and the transfer of control of medical care in prisons to the National Health Service.[7] Yet, there remains a massive gulf between

Judge Tumim's proposals, let alone Inquest and NAPO's, and the stark realities of the inhumane and degrading treatment to which many prisoners are subjected in all forms of custody. Contrast, for example, Judge Tumim's view of the role of the prison officer 'listening, understanding and responding to the needs of inmates',[8] with the following account written in a recent letter to the press by a former inmate:

> The prison medical officers you ask to see at your own risk; foul-mouthed in the extreme, one in particular seemed to enjoy a sadistic pleasure in denying pain killers or treatment. I was told in no uncertain terms that I would find myself on the 'dreaded block' should I make a complaint.
>
> One inmate who some hours earlier had murdered his wife was treated in my view appallingly. On admission, he was greeted with the words 'If you intend to top yourself, do it after eight when I am off duty'; on the officer's tie was a noose with the words 'You know it makes sense'.[9]

Black prisoners face the additional insult of racist taunts and the frequently open displays of racist insignia and right-wing and fascist political propaganda by prison staff. Evidence of such behaviour among prison officers should be made grounds for immediate suspension and dismissal.

Nor is it just people in prison who are denied proper medical treatment. As the cases of those who have died at police stations or in cells at court illustrate all too well, there can be serious neglect by police custody officers, and police surgeons often display a similar incompetence and lack of professional independence to that among prison medical officers. (As we write, two police surgeons have been charged with manslaughter of a remand prisoner who died in a police cell in Grimsby in September 1990.[10]) This, in turn, makes a mockery of the provisions of the official codes of practice for the treatment of those detained in police stations, which require that:

> The custody officer must immediately call the police surgeon (or, in urgent cases, send the person to hospital or call the nearest available medical practitioner) if a person . . .
> (a) appears to be suffering from physical illness or a medical disorder; or
> (b) is injured; or
> (c) does not show signs of sensibility and awareness; or
> (d) fails to respond normally to questions or conversation (otherwise than through drunkenness alone); or
> (e) otherwise appears to need medical attention.[11]

Not only are custody officers lacking in medical training to apply these judgments, but the operational demands and conditions in police stations militate against such humane treatment. Indeed, Judge Tumim's account of prison reception procedures would apply equally to those operating in the charge rooms of most inner-city police stations:

> The priority for reception units is often to process as quickly as possible a large number of prisoners through a small, cramped area and locate them in the main prison with the minimum of disturbance and using as few staff as possible. The process . . . has been described as 'the daily miracle'. Others saw it as a production line. Prison staff who work with receptions are necessarily motivated to complete the important legal processes and to avoid violent confrontations . . . The Circular Instruction [on preventing suicide] takes for granted a quality of care in the way people are received into prison; a routine procedure carried out in haste in unsatisfactory surroundings does not demonstrate this quality of care.[12]

The same can be said of the problems of enforcing the codes of practice applying to the police, although with them there is the additional motivation of giving priority to questioning suspects and obtaining evidence on which to base charges, rather than looking to the medical welfare of detainees.

In the face of the evidence presented here and elsewhere, there is a strong case for a fundamental review, as demanded by Inquest and NAPO, not only of the Prison Medical Service but of the medical treatment accorded to all persons in custody. Such a review should be aimed at establishing an independently-controlled service (most probably as a branch of the National Health Service) with a duty of ensuring the provision of medical care, to the same standards as apply elsewhere, for those held in police stations, prisons and other places of detention. This service would take over control and responsibility for the professional standards of both prison medical officers and police surgeons, the medical training of police custody officers and of nurses in prisons and at special hospitals* and the organisation of adequate emergency medical cover for police stations and prisons on a 24-hour-a-day basis. In prisons or other places of detention of any significant size, this coverage should encompass the presence on site of a fully qualified medical practitioner at all times. At the same time, those held in police stations should have a statutory right, as an alternative to using the 24-hour emergency medical service provided, to obtain treatment or examination by a doctor of their own choice, paid for – as in the case of legal advice – by the state. There should also be a machinery established, possibly through the board of visitors, where prison inmates can also demand a second medical

---

* Inquest and NAPO have recommended that 'hospital officers', who are all members of the Prison Officers' Association, should be replaced by NHS nurses.

opinion from an outside doctor in appropriate cases. Also, the denial or delaying of access to medical assistance for those held in custody by police or prison officers should be made a disciplinary offence punishable by dismissal, and there should be a duty on all concerned to ensure that relevant medical records are passed on immediately to the relevant authorities whenever prisoners are tranferred for any reason.

Finally, there is a need for greater civilian supervision over the conditions in which people are held in custody. It is notable, for example, that boards of visitors have no role at present in prison suicide prevention management groups, and Judge Tumim has recommended that prisoners should also take part in such groups. Also, recent research has shown that police station lay visitor schemes are ineffectual, with members often unsure of what their role is in checking on the treatment of detainees or how far they are able to exercise their rights.[13] Both of these groups need to be given a more structured, positive function, not only in checking on conditions in police stations and prisons, but also as channels for complaints. And where detainees do complain or report maltreatment of themselves or fellow inmates – or, indeed, members of boards of visitors or lay visitor schemes pass on or give publicity to such complaints – the system should provide them with protection against official or unofficial retaliation for doing so.

• **The use of racist language or taunts and the wearing or displaying of racist slogans, insignia or other propaganda (including that of far-right and fascist political organisations) by prison staff during the course of their periods on duty should be made subject to immediate suspension and eventual dismissal from the service.**

• **An independent agency should be established to take over reponsibility for the provision of medical services to all persons held in police or prison custody. The control of both the Prison Medical Service and police surgeons should be passed immediately to this agency, which would then have the duty to provide adequate supervision and training for all police and staff in prisons with medical responsibilities and a system of 24-hour emergency medical coverage for all custodial establishments.**

• **Those held in any form of state custody should have a statutory right to the same standard of medical care as citizens in general and to demand, at state expense, independent examination and treatment by a doctor of their choice. The denial of access to medical assistance by police or prison officers should be made grounds for dismissal.**

• **A more effective system for civilian supervision of conditions in police stations and prisons needs to be established, including the representation of boards of visitors and prisoners on suicide prevention groups in prisons.**

• **Those making, passing on, or publicising complaints of maltreatment in custodial establishments should be given adequate protection against retaliation by staff.**

Holding the custodians to account

No programme for prevention of injury or death of those held in custody will be effective unless it is backed up by an adequate system for holding the custodians – the police, prison officers, hospital staff – accountable for their acts of negligence and maltreatment of those in their care. And no system of discipline will work without its being based on a foundation of rights for detainees themselves and for their families and communities – rights of full disclosure of information, of prompt and independent investigation, of legal representation within the system, and of expeditious redress where neglect has occurred. For, whoever else may be charged with the responsibility for investigating such cases, no one will have the same interest as the family and the community in ensuring that truth is out.

As a priority, therefore, statutory rights of disclosure of all relevant information and materials to the next-of-kin of injured or deceased persons in custody should be established. These rights should encompass Judge Tumim's recent recommendations that it should be prison staff, possibly the governor, rather than the police, who should inform next-of-kin of a death in prison; that next-of-kin should have a right to be present at post mortems and to have a doctor of their own choice present as well; that they or their legal representatives should be 'given access to, or copies of, papers and, if necessary, allowed to visit the actual scene of death'; and that next-of-kin 'should enter the inquest procedure with the same amount of information as the Prison Service'.[14] Each of these recommendations apply with equal, if not greater weight, to the rights and procedures that should apply following a death in a police station, in hospital custody, or in other places of detention. But the right of access to information must also be backed up by adequate resources and help for the deceased person's family to make full use of it. In particular, where a death has occurred to a person in any form of state custody, there should be an automatic right to free legal and medical assistance (without a means test) for the next-of-kin to investigate the matter and to be represented at any subsequent investigatory or disciplinary hearing, inquest or tribunal. It is also essential that lawyers handling such cases should be suitably qualified and trained, and the Law Society should consider establishing a specialist panel of solicitors (similar to that already operating for child care cases) with particular experience in representing families at inquests.

Judge Tumim, drawing on the example of deaths in police custody, has also recommended that the responsibility for investigating deaths in prison should be given to a governor from another establishment. But, as case after case shows, the investigation of deaths in police custody by an officer from a different force, even if 'supervised' by the Police Complaints Authority, is unsatisfactory. And, although there is a need to reform the inquest procedure along the lines recommended by Inquest and other bodies, there are clear limits as to how far such a procedure can go in exposing all the circumstances surrounding a death in custody, where the motive for cover-up by those in authority is so strong.

In these circumstances, there is a strong case for establishing a permanent commission, with independent staff and full investigatory powers, to, in the first instance, examine and prepare a report on the deaths of all persons held in any form of state custody. The commission should also constitute a higher level of tribunal, beyond the coroner's inquest, to determine, following full judicial and public hearings, all the circumstances surrounding a death in custody and, where appropriate, to recommend disciplinary or criminal proceedings against those responsible and compensation for next-of-kin. Although it may not be necessary to hold a full inquiry (as distinct from preparing a preliminary report) on every death in custody, an open system to apply to the commission to do so should be established. For example, coroners, prison boards of visitors, prison welfare groups, fellow prisoners, as well as next-of-kin, should be able to pass on information to the commission in confidence and to demand a full inquiry into any particular death.

• **Statutory rights of access to all relevant information and to free legal and medical assistance should be established for the family of any person seriously injured or who has died while in any form of state custody.**

• **Inquest procedures should be reformed to provide for full disclosure of evidence and legal aid for next-of-kin, for a wider range of verdicts, and to restore juries' right to make recommendations and add riders to verdicts.**

• **The Law Society should establish a specialist panel of solicitors with experience in representing families at inquest proceedings.**

• **A permanent, independent Commission on Deaths in Custody should be established to investigate and prepare a report on the full circumstances surrounding all deaths in any form of state custody and to constitute a higher level tribunal of inquiry into such cases. Access to the commission should be on an open basis to all interested parties.**

Black people and the criminal justice system

According to Home Office statistics, the proportion of black* prisoners in British jails (as at June 1990) was 15.9 per cent. For men, the figure was 15.5 per cent, for women 25.8 per cent.[1] And yet, black people comprise some 4.4 per cent of the population, according to the latest census information. In some particular establishments based in inner-city areas, the proportion of black prisoners is even higher. As at June 1988, 23.6 per cent of prisoners at Brixton were of West Indian/ Guyanese or African descent, 29 per cent at Holloway, 25.5 per cent at Wormwood Scrubs, 13.8 per cent at Birmingham.[2]

The reasons that, proportionately, so many more black than white people end up in prison are many. First, evidence shows that there is a particular policing practice being used where the black community is concerned.[3] Black areas and black events are often over-policed, particular crimes are associated with black young people – hence special squads with special tactics are more widely used in black areas. A study by Carole Willis found that young black men aged 16-24 were stopped roughly 10 times more frequently than the average for the population.[4] A survey by the Policy Studies Institute in 1983 found that 63 per cent of West Indian men aged 15-24 had been stopped by the Metropolitan Police.[5]

There is also evidence to suggest that certain crimes are more likely to be reported to the police, and therefore investigated, than others. A 1984 study concluded that the likelihood of victims reporting crimes was affected by their perception of the ethnic origin of the perpetrator.[6]

Second, decisions by the police regarding the treatment of juvenile offenders differ according to race. For public order offences, auto-crimes and crimes of violence, white juveniles are twice as likely to be cautioned as their black counterparts and a white juvenile with previous convictions is over four times more likely to be cautioned than his/her black counterpart. The National Association for the Care and Rehabilitation of Offenders (NACRO) believes that: 'The proportion of young

---

* The Home Office Prisons Department uses the term black to include West Indian, Guyanese, African, Indian, Pakistani, Bangladeshi, Chinese, Arab and mixed origin – and is so used here.

Black men going into custody is twice as high as the proportion of young white men, this means that nearly one in 10 of the young men in the Black community will have been locked up by his twenty-first birthday.'[7]

Third, those juveniles who reach the court system are again treated differentially. An unpublished survey of 2,000 defendants aged 17 to 21 appearing at Birmingham Magistrates' Court in 1979 found that defendants of West Indian origin were nearly twice as likely to be committed to Crown Court as their white counterparts. And a more recent Hackney study of juvenile courts found that fewer black young people were acquitted than white and that custodial sentences were being used twice as frequently.[8] According to NACRO, young black persons appear to be over-represented amongst those sentenced to a period of detention under section 53 of the 1933 Children's Act.[9]

It appears from a study of the south-east London Probation Service that Afro-Caribbeans serving youth custody orders are less likely to have had previous convictions, less likely to have been on probation previously and come from more stable homes than their white counterparts.[10] A monitoring of the West Midlands Probation Service in 1986 showed that black defendants were more likely to get an immediate or suspended custodial sentence than a community service order, a fine or supervision or probation order than their white counterparts.[11] This finding was corroborated by other research by the Home Office.[12]

Fourth, evidence suggests that black defendants are more likely to be held in custody to await trial than white defendants. And, since a higher proportion of black defendants who are remanded are subsequently acquitted than white defendants, it suggests that blacks are being inappropriately remanded in custody in the first place.[13]

Fifth, when black people are sentenced, they appear to be given longer terms on average than their white counterparts. Though this is very hard to establish categorically, matching offence to offence, it is clear from the Home Office figures of the terms served by black and white prisoners in 1989 that, whereas black men make up only 10.5 per cent of those serving 18 months and under, they make up 16.5 per cent of those serving over 18 months. For black women, the figures are even more striking. They comprise 14.2 per cent of those serving 18 months or less, but 34.2 per cent of those serving 18 months or more.

Black people also end up in disproportionate numbers in the custodial care of psychiatric hospitals. A 1977 study found that 494 people per 100,000 born here were admitted to mental hospital as compared with 539 per 100,000 of those born in the Caribbean. Another study in southern England found black people were three times more likely than whites to be admitted for schizophrenia.[14] There is no space here to cover the debate about the misdiagnosis and maltreatment of black people in the psychiatric system in general. Besides, it has been written up elsewhere.[15]

What is relevant, however, is the fact that a greater proportion of black people than white are 'sectioned' – i.e., compulsorily referred to hospitals by courts, the police, and the Home Secretary under the Mental Health Act. Sections 35, 36, 37 and 38 of Part III of the 1983 Mental Health Act allow the courts to remand defendants to hospital for reports, to commit convicted persons to hospital or make them subject to a guardianship order. Sections 47 and 48 enpower the Home Secretary to transfer a convicted prisoner or a remanded prisoner from prison to be detained in hospital. Under section 136, the police can remove to a psychiatric hospital anyone found in a place to which the public has access and who appears to be suffering from a mental disorder and in need of care or control.

An analysis of Home Office figures for the Metropolitan Police District (1984/85) found that 36 per cent of those given hospital orders with restrictions were known to be black; 32 per cent of people given hospital orders (without restrictions) were black.[16] A more recent study found that young Afro-Caribbeans born in the Caribbean are up to 25 times more likely than whites to be committed for detention under Part III of the Act.[17]

References

Chapter 1

1 *Police against black people* (London, Institute of Race Relations, 1979) and *Policing against black people* (London, Institute of Race Relations, 1987).
2 Information on David Oluwale's life and death taken from Ron Phillips, 'The death of one lame darkie', *Race Today* (January 1972) and Jeremy Sandford, *Smiling David: the story of David Oluwale* (London, Calder and Boyars, 1974).
3 As quoted in Phillips, ibid.
4 Ibid.
5 Ibid.
6 Ibid.
7 Ibid.
8 Ibid.
9 Ibid.
10 *Caribbean Times* (30.9.88, 28.10.88 and 14.4.89); *Voice* (25.4.89).
11 *Northampton Post* (16.10.87); *Voice* (20.10.87); *Caribbean Times* (23.10.87 and 27.11.87).
12 *Policing against black people*, op. cit., pp 22-27.
13 *The Broadwater Farm Inquiry* (London, Karia Press, 1986), Chapter 4.
14 As quoted in ibid.
15 *Race Today* (July 1987); *Searchlight* (December 1988); *Caribbean Times* (4.11.88); *IRR Police-Media Bulletin* (Nos. 30, 32, 42, and 46).
16 *Race Today* (July 1987).
17 *Caribbean Times* (4.11.88).
18 CARF, 'McCurbin inquest verdict condemned', *Searchlight* (December 1988).
19 *Abolitionist* (Nos. 21 and 22, 1986); *Policing London* (September/October 1986); *Times* (16.12.86); *Independent* (11.2.87); *Guardian* (20.2.87); *IRR Police-Media Bulletin* (Nos 21, 22, 27, 29, 32 and 33).
20 *Abolitionist*, ibid.
21 *Middlesex Chronicle* (31.12.86).
22 *Guardian* (20.2.87).
23 *Black Voice* (Vol. 12, no. 13); *Sunday Times* (11.7.82); *Searchlight* (September and December 1981); *Caribbean Times* (13.2.90).
24 Phil Scraton and Kathryn Chadwick, *In the arms of the law* (London, Pluto, 1986); *South East London Mercury* (19.5.83, 21.7.83); *Daily Telegraph* (12.7.83); *Guardian* (16.7.83); *Scotsman* (16.7.83).
25 *Caribbean Times* (28.1.88); *Voice* (19.1.88); *Hackney Gazette* (3.7.87); *Searchlight* (September 1987); *IRR Police-Media Bulletin* (Nos. 35 and 40).
26 Interview in *Hurriyet*, quoted in *City Limits* (10.12.87).
27 *Voice* (19.1.88).
28 Quoted in *IRR Police-Media Bulletin* (No. 40).
29 *City Limits* (28.1.88).

30 *City Limits* (8.2.89); *Voice* (11.7.89); *Caribbean Times* (14.7.89, 21.7.89,28.7.89).
31 Melissa Benn and Ken Worpole, *Death in the city* (London, Canary Press, 1986) ; 'Who killed Aseta Simms', *Black Voice* (Vol. 2, no. 4).
32 As quoted in *Death in the city*, ibid.
33 *Daily Telegraph* (24.3.83); *Morning Star* (24.3.83).
34 *Evening Standard* (23.5.85); *South London Press* (7.11.86).
35 *Grassroots* (February-March 1979); *Policing in Hackney: a record of HCRE's experiences 1978-82* (London, HCRE, 1983).
36 *Observer* (3.5.87); *Searchlight* (May 1987).
37 *Searchlight* (May 1987).
38 *Caribbean Times* (30.1.87); *Romford and Hornchurch Recorder* (30.1.87); *Guardian* (30.1.87); Hackney Legal Defence Committee letter to Police Complaints Authority, undated.
39 As quoted in *Caribbean Times* (30.1.87).

Chapter 2

1 Andrew Rutherford, 'First reform your staff', *Independent* (10.4.91) and *Cmnd 1383 Report of a Review by Her Majesty's Chief Inspector of Prisons for England and Wales of Suicide and Self-harm in Prison Establishments in England and Wales* (London, HMSO, 1990).
2 *Caribbean Times* (4.12.87); *Voice* (1.12.87); *Searchlight* (November 1987); *IRR Police-Media Bulletin* (No. 40).
3 *Inquiry into the death of Armando Belonia*, Wandsworth Prison Board of Visitors, February, 1989; Sarah Boseley, 'Care and punishment', *Guardian* (25.7.90); *Guardian* (25.6.88).
4 Wandsworth Board of Visitors Inquiry Report, op. cit., p.14.
5 *Guardian* (25.6.88).
6 Letter from Douglas Hogg, Parliamentary Under Secretary of State, Home Office (29.9.88).
7 Wandsworth Board of Visitors Inquiry Report, op. cit., pp 20-23.
8 *Abolitionist* (No. 23, 1987).
9 *Time Out* (29.6.88).
10 As quoted in ibid.
11 Ibid.
12 Ibid.
13 *Death of Richard 'Cartoon' Campbell* (London, Battersea and Wandsworth Trades Council, 1981); *Westindian World* (17.4.80, 27.7.80); *New Statesman* (4.7.80); *Grassroots* (May-June 1980).
14 Battersea and Wandsworth Trades Council, op. cit., p.3.
15 Ibid., p.14.
16 Ibid., p.15
17 Ibid.
18 Ibid., p.16.
19 Phil Scraton, op.cit.
20 *Westindian World* (4.1.74).
21 As quoted in ibid.
22 As quoted in ibid.

23 Brixton Defence Campaign (No. 4); *City Limits* (30.1.89); *Guardian* *(25.7.90)*.
24 *Guardian* (25.7.90).
25 Ibid.
26 *Guardian* (25.10.90); *Eastern Eye* (13.11.90); *Derbyshire Evening Telegraph* (27.10.90).
27 *Guardian* (25.10.90).
28 Ibid.
29 *Derbyshire Evening Telegraph* (27.10.90).
30 *Guardian* (8.3.91); *Observer* (17.3.91); Inquest proceedings.
31 *Inquest Annual Report 1986-87; Voice* (7.7.87); *Searchlight* (September 1987); *Guardian* (3.7.87).
32 *Guardian* (3.7.87).
33 *Inquest Annual Report, 1986-87.*
34 Accounts related by refugee workers.
35 *Asian Times* (24.6.88); *Glasgow Evening Times* (20.7.89).
36 *Shepherds Bush-Hammersmith Gazette* (10.7.87); *Searchlight* (May 1987).
37 *Shepherds Bush-Hammersmith Gazette* (10.7.87).
38 *Independent* (13.4.90); *Guardian* (13.4.90); *Caribbean Times* (17.4.90); *Time Out* (20.1.90, 7.2.90); *Living Marxism* (February 1990); Inquest.
39 *Time Out* (7.2.90).
40 *Guardian* (13.4.90).
41 *Independent* (13.4.90).

Chapter 3

1 Errol Francis, 'Black people, "dangerousness" and psychiatric compulsion', in Anny Brackx and Catherine Grimshaw (eds), *Mental health care in crisis* (London, Pluto, 1989); CARF, 'Mad or bad: interview with Errol Francis', *Searchlight* (April 1990).
2 Black Health Workers' and Patients' Group, 'Psychiatry and the corporate state', *Race & Class* (Vol. XXV, No. 2, Autumn 1983).
3 R. Cope, 'The compulsory detention of Afro-Caribbeans under the Mental Health Act', *New Community* (April 1989).
4 *Guardian* (26.4.91 and 5.6.91).
5 'Special Hospital', *Cutting Edge* (20/20 Vision, 4.3.91).
6 Errol Francis, 'How did Michael Martin Die?', *Open Mind* (No. 13, Feb-March 1985); Errol Francis, 'Death at Broadmoor – brutality exposed', *Searchlight* (June 1985); *Report to the Secretary of State for Social Services concerning the Death of Michael Dean Martin at Broadmoor Hospital on 6 July 1984*, the Ritchie Report (Department of Health and Social Security, 1985); *Glasgow Herald* (2.9.85); *South London Press* (6.9.85); *Daily Telegraph* (31.8.85).
7 Ritchie Report, op. cit., p. 2.
8 Ibid.
9 Ibid., p. 4.
10 Ibid., p. 2.
11 'Death at Broadmoor', op.cit.
12 Ritchie Report, op. cit. pp 8-9.

13   Ibid., Appendix 8, p. 1.
14   *Voice* (24.1.87).
15   *Voice* (20.12.88); *Report of the Inquiry into the circumstances leading to the Death in Broadmoor Hospital of Mr Joseph Watts on 23 August 1988* (Special Hospital Service Authority, July 1989).
16   *Report on Joseph Watts*, ibid., p. 6.
17   Ibid.
18   Ibid., p. 11.
19   *Voice* (20.12.88).
20   *Report on Joseph Watts*, op. cit., p. 16.
21   Ibid., p. 17.
22   Ibid., p. 18.
23   *Searchlight* (August 1985).
24   Ibid.

Chapter 5

1   In particular, Review of Suicide and Self-harm, op. cit., and *Report on HM Prison Brixton by HM Chief Inspector of Prisons* (London, Home Office, 1990).
2   Sir Montague Levine, Southwark Coroner, made five recommendations to be sent to the Home Office following the death of Edwin Robinson (*Guardian*, 6.4.91); Dr Paul Knapman, Westminster Coroner, made three recommendations to be passed to the director of the Prison Medical Services, the suicide prevention management group and the governor of Wandsworth, following the death of Delroy McKnight (inquest 7.3.91).
3   *Police against black people*, op. cit.
4   *Review of suicide and self-harm*, op. cit., para. 373.
5   *Guardian* (6.4.91, 4.5.91).
6   *Review of suicide and self-harm*, op. cit.
7   A campaign to abolish the Prison Medical Service which includes a draft for a Health Care of Prisoners bill, was launched by Inquest and the National Association of Probation Officers in May 1991.
8   *Review of suicide and self-harm*, op. cit.
9   *Independent* (30.4.91).
10   *Times* (2.5.91).
11   Police and Criminal Evidence Act, 1984, Codes of Practice, para. 9.2.
12   *Review of suicide and self-harm*, op. cit., para. 3.05.
13   C.Kemp and R Morgan, 'Lay visitors to police stations' (University of Bristol, 1990).
14   *Review of suicide and self-harm*, op. cit., para. 5.09. In this respect, Judge Tumim adopted part of the recommendations for greater disclosure put to him by Inquest.

Appendix

1   'Table 1: Population in prison establishments at end of month: by sex and ethnic origin, June 1985-June 1990' (Home Office Prisons Department).

2   Population in individual Prison Department establishments by ethnic origin on 30 June 1988 (Written parliamentary answer from Douglas Hogg, Parliamentary Under-Secretary of State at the Home Office, to Barry Sheerman MP, 1 March 1989).
3   See *Policing against Black people*, op. cit.
4   Carole F. Willis, *The use, effectiveness and impact of police stop and search powers* (London, Home Office Research Unit, April 1983).
5   David J. Smith, *Police and people in London* (London, Policy Studies Institute, 1983).
6   K. Pease, *Crime, race and reporting to the police* (Manchester, Manchester University, 1984).
7   *Race and criminal justice* (London, NACRO, 1989).
8   Jonathan Tipler, *Juvenile justice in Hackney* (London, Research Development and Programming Section, Hackney Social Services Directorate, 1985).
9   See *Grave Doubts, Grave Crimes* (London, NACRO, 1988) quoted in *Racism, representation and the criminal justice system* (London, NAPO, 1988).
10 Quoted in 'Some facts and findings about black people in the criminal justice system' (London, NACRO Briefing 77, n.d.).
11 West Midlands Probation Service, 'Report on the Birmingham Court Social Enquiry Report Monitoring Exercise, February 1987'.
12 *Sentencing practice in the Crown Court* (No. 103, HMSO, 1988).
13 Home Office, *Statistical Bulletin 6/89* and Andy Shallice and Paul Gordon, *Black People, White Justice? race and the criminal justice system* (London, Runnymede Trust, 1990).
14 Studies cited in Deryck Browne, *Black people, mental health and the courts* (London, NACRO, 1990).
15 See Errol Francis, op. cit., and Black Health Workers' and Patients' Group, op. cit.
16 Cited in Browne, op. cit.
17 R. Cope, op. cit.

INQUEST

Ground floor, Alexander National House,
330 Seven Sisters Road,
London N4 2PJ

Inquest exists to campaign against deaths in custody and for changes in the coroners' court system. It provides advice and support for families who want to know how and why their relatives died.

If you need help, or if you would like to support the work of Inquest, ring:-
081-802 7430/7450